Time, Space, and Value

Time, Space, and Value

The Narrative Structure
of the *New Arcadia*

Arthur K. Amos, Jr.

Lewisburg
Bucknell University Press
London: Associated University Presses

©1977 by Associated University Presses, Inc.

Associated University Presses, Inc.
Cranbury, New Jersey 08512

Associated University Presses
Magdalen House
136-148 Tooley Street
London SE1 2TT, England

Library of Congress Cataloging in Publication Data

Amos, Arthur K. 1942 –
Time, Space, and Value.

Bibliography: p.
Includes index.
✓ 1. Sidney, Philip, Sr., 1554-1586. The Countess of
Pembroke's Arcadia. 1. Title.
PR2342.A6A4   823'.3   74-30862
ISBN 0-8387-1614-8

PRINTED IN THE UNITED STATES OF AMERICA

For Waldo

Contents

Acknowledgments

Regardless of the half-truths promulgated by title pages, academic works are seldom the work of a single mind. This one surely is not. It, and I, owe debts beyond our ability to repay. Waldo McNeir saw this work through its inception, in general by introducing me to Renaissance literature and in particular by seeing this project through its fledgling drafts. I hope that at least some of his wisdom and humanity shows through my prose. William Cadbury has a share of this too; he introduced me to ways of reading works that go beyond particular periods or people. Thelma Greenfield's contribution is the element of sanity she insisted on in the face of some of my more outrageous assertions.

My colleagues offered encouragement and advice without which this project would never have been completed. The late Linda Van Norden read an early draft of the manuscript and urged me on. Celeste Turner Wright also read the manuscript with diligence and pointed out to me some of my more graceless expressions, most of which I hope I have removed.

Whatever merit this work has would not be here were it

not for the challenge and interest of my Renaissance students at Davis. Two in particular have otherwise unacknowledged contributions: Robert Davis and Elin Diamond. Bob helped me with my share of editing the *Arcadia* and pointed out some aspects of the work that I had not noticed. Elin also worked on the editing and she read critically the manuscript of this work.

Elaine Bukhari typed many drafts and partial drafts of this work. But she did far more than type; she pointed out errors of fact and of expression. Her diligence makes this a far better work than it could otherwise be.

Finally, I am indebted to the staffs at the libraries of the Universities of Oregon and California at Davis, to the staffs of Bucknell University Press and Associated University Presses, Inc., and to all those scholars and critics with whom I take issue but to whom I am indebted far more than I can ever take issue.

Time, Space,
and Value

1
Introduction

i

When Sidney died at Arnheim in 1587, he left behind the
material for critical controversies that may never be completely settled. On the one hand, we find manuscripts of the
Old Arcadia, which had probably been completed by 1580,[1]
and, on the other, we find the incomplete revision of the
earlier work, which has come to be called the *New Arcadia*.[2]
Because the latter work comes to us in an incomplete state,
and because Sidney left no documents to which we may turn
for enlightenment, we have no sure way of knowing what his
attitudes toward the works were. Instead we are obligated
to rely on conjectures based on careful readings of both
Arcadias and on such ancillary sources as Greville's *The Life
of the Renowned Sir Philip Sidney*.[3] Even at that, our prob-

13

lems are compounded by the fact that we have two versions of the *New Arcadia* with which to deal: the version published in quarto under the auspices of Fulke Greville in 1590 and the version of 1593, which is based on, and is substantially the same as, the edition of 1590 and was published under the auspices of Mary Herbert, Countess of Pembroke.[4] The questions that arise from this curious situation include the following: How did Sidney regard the *Old Arcadia* and why did he undertake the revision? How did he regard the revision and why does it break off in mid-sentence? None of these questions can be answered with a high degree of certainty; all we know for sure is that Sidney did decide to revise and recast and that he was either unable or unwilling to complete the task.

There are nonetheless some salient facts to consider in dealing with these questions, not the least of which are Sidney's own remarks on the *Old Arcadia*. In the prefatory letter to Mary, he refers to the *Old Arcadia* as "Being but a trifle, and that triflingly handled" (*OA*, p. 3) and in a letter dated 18 October 1580 to his brother, Robert, he refers to it as "My toyfull booke" (III, 132). These remarks must be used only with extreme caution, however, as we may be sure that Sidney spoke of his "trifle" with carefully cultivated *sprezzatura*. Modern study of the *Old Arcadia*, moreover, has concluded that it is a highly moral, artful narrative that teaches and delights.[5] Nevertheless, without denigrating the *Old Arcadia*, and without necessarily agreeing with Sidney, we might say that there is an undertone of seriousness to his claim regarding the *Old Arcadia* that "in itself it have deformities" (*OA*, p. 3). Perhaps, after reading parts of it to the Earl of Angus and hearing complaints like Thomas Howell's, that it had been kept from circulation "all to[o] long,"[6] he began to consider possible publication, to revise his work, and to correct the "deformities." We shall never know.

We can see, however, possible "deformities" that Sidney may have wanted to correct in the revised version. One of these is the relationship of the narrator to his characters. In the *Old Arcadia*, the narrator regards the princes with slightly amused, slightly critical tolerance; although Pyrocles and Musidorus are the heroes of the work, with all the positive attributes that the word *hero* implies, the folly of their behavior also receives much weight. Though their follies are forgivable and in human terms fully understandable, the heroes are ethically ambiguous and therefore less than ideal, a fact about which the narrator makes no bones. In spite of their follies and in spite of the follies of Basilius and Gynecia, all turns out well — the princes marry the princesses and, presumably, everyone lives happily ever after. The narrator's critical stance serves as an ethical corrective of the view that rewards come despite folly — a view that might seem to follow naturally the comic structure of the *Old Arcadia*. In the *New Arcadia*, Pyrocles and Musidorus are more fully idealized, less foolish. They take their values from what they have learned in their adventures in Asia Minor (Book II) as well as from the idealism implicit in the pastoral, Arcadian setting. As a result there is no need for the narrator to provide an ethical corrective and he is therefore less distanced from his protagonists than in the earlier work.

A second difference between the *Old Arcadia* and the *New Arcadia*, not unconnected with the stance of the narrator, has to do with the way in which the two works are didactic. In the *Old Arcadia* teaching is a primary function of the narrator. In the *New Arcadia*, the didactic component arises out of the parallels between events and between characters. In many ways, it seems as if Sidney uses his episodes to suggest various permutations of vices and virtues. Thus, in Book I circling around Pyrocles' love for Philoclea and Musidorus's for Pamela are episodes involving fully idealized love (Argalus and Parthenia), affected love (Phalantus and Artesia), adulterous love (Basilius for "Zelmane" and Gynecia for Pyrocles), sheer lust (Demagoras for Parthenia), and opposition to love (Musidorus's lecture to Pyrocles). In a similar way, Sidney suggests permutations in the political and heroic spheres.

The didacticism of the later work arises out of the combination of negative and positive *exempla* and therefore shares characteristics with other of what Northrop Frye calls the encyclopedic and anatomical forms.[7]

If both these changes suggest "deformities" that Sidney wished to correct, they also suggest an expansion of purpose. John Buxton, for example, argues that Sidney thought of himself as doing something far more radical in his revision than merely converting a straightforward story into an intricate romance patterned after Heliodorus. He was producing "something that must invite comparison with the *Aeneid* and *The Faerie Queene*. For him, as for Spenser, as for Milton, as for Dryden, the heroic poem was a poem with a moral purpose."[8] Although Buxton rather slights the moral component of the *Old Arcadia* more than he ought, he is surely right in his suggestion that Sidney probably saw the *New Arcadia* as different in kind from the *Old Arcadia*. As one of the *Old Arcadia's* most sympathetic readers, Richard Lanham, puts it: "Perhaps we should expect a work revised to be not a better version of the same thing, but something basically different and more ambitious."[9] In part, this greater ambition is reflected in the increased emphasis on political and heroic materials and in part in the increased complexity of the narrative structure of the later work. Whereas the *Old Arcadia* is basically linear in its narrative structure, the *New Arcadia* is basically convoluted, ever turning back on itself. And this convoluted structure is particularly appropriate to the thematic interests of the work just as the linear approach is appropriate to the concerns of the *Old Arcadia*.

ii

The publication in 1965 of Walter Davis's *Map of Arcadia: Sidney's Romance in Its Tradition* and Richard Lanham's *The Old "Arcadia"* marks the beginning of new directions in the study of Sidney's prose works.[10] Prior to their studies, scholars had devoted themselves almost exclusively to such matters as sources of the two works, the relationships between the texts, possible incidences of historical allegory in each, and the relative worth of each.[11] While these issues continue to be discussed, *Arcadian* criticism since Davis and Lanham has focused on thematic issues and on genre identification. Critics have realized that the *Old* and *New Arcadias* ought to be treated as separate, though related, works.

Even with this shift in criticism, too little attention has been paid to the narrative structure of the *New Arcadia* other than noting its complexity and some of the parallels between episodes. In a way, Virginia Woolf's attack on the narrative structure of Sidney's work has remained unanswered and has even been echoed in different terms by some otherwise excellent and exciting recent criticism; as she put it: "... Sidney seized his pen too carelessly. He had no notion when he set out where he was going. Telling stories, he thought, was enough — one could follow another interminably. But where there is no end in view there is no sense of direction to draw us on."[12] A careful study of the structure of the *New Arcadia* strongly suggests otherwise. Such a study, moreover, might also help us to avoid some of the problems implicit in any study that begins with an *a priori* assumption of thematic interest such as Davis's or of generic form such as Lawry's, since both theme and genre ought to be deduced from structure.

The *New Arcadia* makes use of two basic structural principles. One of these involves the use of parallel episodes to work out permutations of particular vices and virtues. To a large extent, the parallel episodes function to establish the range of the thematic cores of the work, which may be baldly divided into the areas of public and private behavior. In the public realm, the emphasis is politics: the appropriate balance between rulers and subjects, and this includes the weighing of the privileges and responsibilities of both. In the realm of private behavior, the emphasis is on the problems raised by erotic attractions. Instead of imposing a sense of discontinuity between the two kinds of behavior, however, Sidney's fiction shows that they are fundamentally interrelated; a private action can and often does have public consequences while political acts often influence private behavior. The interrelationship between the two modes of behavior suggests the significance of chivalric and heroic codes of conduct since these, like Sidney's narrative, cut across the artificial boundary lines implied by the terms *public* and *private*. In all the areas of behavior with which the *New Arcadia* deals, moreover, it tends to undercut absolutist systems: particular situations, the work implies, determine how the abstract rules of politics, ethics, and chivalry are to be applied.

Though critics have noted the interrelationship between some of the episodes of the *New Arcadia,* they have paid little or no attention to the second and overriding structural principle of the work. The *New Arcadia* is made up of two complete books and part of a third; presumably it would have had five books if it had been completed. The unspoken assumption is that the five-book structure is a carryover from the five-act, Terentian structure of the *Old Arcadia.* A careful examination, however, reveals that each of the three books of the *New Arcadia* has its own ordering principle; these are, respectively, the dyadic relationships of space (here, there, in front of), time (then or now, before or after), and value (better or worse).[13] These relationships are, of course, central ways of organizing experience and each of the three books tends to emphasize one of the three relationships.

Book I is marked by its pictorial quality, which corresponds to spatial ordering. Much of what goes on in this book contributes directly to building a theory of perceptual psychology, the rudiments of which are concerned with the way the individual perceives the world and how he acts on those perceptions. The theory is Janus-faced; the way an individual feels and acts determines what he sees, and what he sees determines the way he feels and acts. Pyrocles reshapes Arcadia into an idealized landscape when he falls in love with Philoclea; Strephon and Claius reshape it into a wasteland after their love, Urania, leaves. For Sidney, the world and the self are not discrete but exist in a perceptual continuum. This fact has ramifications for art both within and without the narrative. Within the narrative, Pryocles can fall in love with a portrait of Philoclea just as if it were the girl herself. We may recall that for Sidney the function of poetry, as presumably the other arts as well, is "to teach and delight" (III, 9). But teaching is not an end in itself, "for as *Aristotle* saith, it is not [*gnosis*] but [*praxis*] must be the frute: and how [*praxis*] can be without being moved to practise, it is no hard matter to consider" (III, 19). Philoclea's portrait, then, fulfills the function of art in that it moves Pyrocles to love and, we presume, love virtuously. We may further suggest that there is an analoguous relationship between the *New Arcadia* and the reader; it too will move the reader to act virtuously by moving the reader to imitate the virtues of Pyrocles and Musidorus. Nonetheless, the perceptual theory underlying Book I risks two rather serious dangers: too much stress on the power of the world to influence the self leads to naturalistic overdetermination and too much emphasis on the power of the individual to create what he sees leads to sheer solipsism. Sidney steers a straight course between this Charybdis and this Scylla but his means of doing so remain unclear until the added dimensions of time and value are revealed in Books II and III.

The pictorial quality pervading most of Book I is considerably subdued in Book II, where the narrative becomes less linear and more convoluted. As a result, the emphasis shifts from spatial relationships to temporal relationships; events are placed in time as well as space. The events covered range from a period before the births of Pyrocles and Musidorus to the declarations of love by Pyrocles and Philoclea and to the implication that Pamela returns Musidorus's love. Since, however, the advance in time between the events in the main narrative at the end of Book I and those at the end of Book II is comparatively small, the emphasis falls on the causal relationship between events in the past and those in the present.

The book tends to show that causal sequences move geometrically in either direction from single events, so that a single event will have a plurality of both causes and effects. Significance is derived from the placement in time and causality. The weight placed on complex, multiple causality is reflected in the book by the complexity of the narrative itself.

Book III of the *New Arcadia*, finally, differs from the previous two books in that it emphasizes the problem of norms. In it the primary thematic tension arises from the conflict of alternative value systems, between the protagonists' values and Cecropia's. Neither side, however, feels any real threat to its system; each remains convinced that its own values are efficacious. The tension between the two is felt most strongly by Amphialus, who can neither accept his mother's values nor act upon his beloved's. Since much of the narrative of Book III is devoted to his ambivalent feelings, the audience feels the strength of the conflict, but always prefers the values held by Pyrocles, Musidorus, and the two princesses to those held by Cecropia. The debates among the three women, moreover, tend to suggest a way of adjudicating between alternative values: because the system of Philoclea and Pamela encompasses not only Cecropia's values but other, theistically oriented values as well, the better value system appears to be the one that incorporates the greatest good. The second test of values implicit in Book III is pragmatic and temporal: of opposing value systems, the system with bad consequences (promiscuity, political chaos, damnation) is less desirable than one that avoids these evil consequences. The tests of values in the *New Arcadia*, then, undercut absolutism even in matters of ethical codes. Thus Pamela, perhaps the most "upright" of the four central characters, errs when she proposes suicide after rigorously applying her own values to the situation in which she finds herself when Anaxius takes over Amphialus's castle.

The two structural principles that I have suggested here underscore the thematic range of the *New Arcadia* as well as its means of organizing the material included within that range. If one were to generalize at this point, he might go so far as to suggest that the thematic range is human behavior itself in all its complexity and that the means of organizing are essentially the same means as we use today. The inference is obvious: although the world of the *New Arcadia* seems at first blush to be distant and alien to our own, neither its fundamental concerns nor its means of treating those concerns is distant or alien. In a sense the work is of a modern temper as well as of a Renaissance one.

Notes

1. Evidence for this date is summarized in *The Poems of Sir Philip Sidney,* ed. William A. Ringler, Jr. (Oxford, 1962), pp. 364-66. Cited as *Poems.*

2. Here, and in succeeding chapters when the distinction must be maintained, the composite text published in 1593 by Mary Herbert, Countess of Pembroke, is called the *Arcadia;* the early form of the work not published until this century, the *Old Arcadia;* and the portion of the *Arcadia* on which Sidney apparently completed his revision, the *New Arcadia.* Where there is no chance of confusion — that is, where the difference between the incomplete revision and the composite text is not significant, as in the middle three chapters of what follows — the title *Arcadia* applies to both versions of the revised work, the 1590 and 1593 editions. I have used for my Arcadian material a photocopy of the Huntington Library copy of the 1593 edition. My quotations are modernized in accord with a projected modern-spelling edition of the *Arcadia* by Professors James Hallerin, William Jones, Michael Payne, and myself. The quotations have been collated with a photocopy of the Folger Library copy of the 1593 edition, with the H. Oskar Sommer fascimile of the 1590 quarto (London, 1891; reprinted with the excellent introduction of Carl Dennis [Kent, Ohio, 1970]), with copies of the folios of 1598 and 1613, and with the edition of the Prose Works edited by Albert Feuillerat,.4 vols. (Cambridge, England, 1962; reprinted from the 5-volume *Complete Works,* 1912). For the convenience of those readers who do not have access to the 1593 edition I have made the page references in my text to the *Arcadia,* as well as to the non-Arcadian prose, agree with the Feuillerat edition. Citations from the *Old Arcadia* are to Jean Robertson's edition (Oxford, 1973). The definitive edition of the poetry is Ringler's and citations from the non-Arcadian poems are to it.

3. Ed. Nowell Smith (Oxford, 1907).

4. In addition to Ringler's discussion of textual matters, one should look at: R. W. Zandvoort, *Sidney's "Arcadia": A Comparison between the Two Versions* (Amsterdam, 1929), pp. 1-41; Kenneth O. Myrick, *Sir Philip Sidney as*

a Literary Craftsman (Cambridge, Mass., 1939; Lincoln, Neb., 1965), pp. 112-13;
Kenneth T. Rowe, "The Countess of Pembroke's Editorship of the *Arcadia*,"
PMLA 54 (1939); 122-38; Leigh Godshalk, "Sidney's Revision of the *Arcadia*,"
Books III-V" *PQ* 63 (1964): 171-84; Joan Rees, "Fulke Greville and the Revisions
of *Arcadia*," *RES* 17 (1966): 54-57; and Peter Lindenbaum, "Sidney's *Arcadia*:
The Endings of the Three Versions," *HLQ* 34 (1971): 205-28.

5. This claim is strongly made by Richard A. Lanham in his ground-breaking
The Old "Arcadia," Sidney's Arcadia, *YSE* 158 (New Haven, Conn., 1965), pp.
181-410. It has been supported by Elizabeth Dipple, " 'Unjust Justice' in the
Old Arcadia," *SEL* 10 (1970): 83-101 and "Harmony and Pastoral in the Old
Arcadia," *ELH* 35 (1968): 309-28; Franco Marenco, *Arcadia Puritana: L'uso della
tradizione nella prima "Arcadia" di Sir Philip Sidney* (Bari, 1968) and "Double
Plot in Sidney's Old *Arcadia*," *MLR* 64 (1969); 248-63; Robert W. Parker, "Ter-
entian Structure and Sidney's Original *Arcadia*," *ELR* 2 (1972); 61-78; and Jon
S. Lawry, *Sidney's Two Arcadias: Pattern and Proceeding* (Ithaca, N.Y., 1972),
pp. 16-153.

6. Holinshed, *Chronicles* (1587 uncensored version), p. 1554 and cited in
Poems, p. 365. The brackets are Ringler's.

7. See his discussion of these forms in the *Anatomy of Criticism: Four
Essays* (Princeton, N. J., 1957), pp. 308-26.

8. *Elizabethan Taste* (New York, 1964), pp. 255-56.

9. *The Old "Arcadia,"* p. 395.

10. These two studies are combined in *Sidney's Arcadia, Yale Studies in
English*, 158. Their work has been succeeded by Mark Rose, *Heroic Love: Studies
in Sidney and Spenser* (Cambridge, Mass., 1968); Robert Kimbrough, *Sir Philip
Sidney*, Twane's English Author Series 114 (New York, 1971); and a rather long
list of articles for which see Mary A. Washington, *Sir Philip Sidney: An Annotated
Bibliography of Modern Criticism, 1941-1970* (Columbia, Mo. 1972) and William
L. Godshalk, "Recent Sutdies in Sidney," *ELR* 2 (1972): 148-64. It should be
mentioned in passing that the Winter number of *ELR* 2 (1972) is devoted to
studies of Sidney's works.

11. Studies dealing with the problem of sources include S. L. Wolff, *The
Greek Romances in Elizabethan Prose Fiction* (New York, 1912); T. P. Harrison,
"A Source of Sidney's *Arcadia*," University of Texas *Studies in English* 6 (1926):
53-71; Marcus Seldon Goldman, "Malory's *Morte d'Arthur* in the *Arcadia*," *Sir
Philip Sidney and the "Arcadia,"* Illinois Studies in Language and Literature, 17,
nos. 1-2 (Urbana, Ill., 1934): Freda Townsend, "Sidney and Ariosto," *PMLA* 61
(1946): 97-108; Mary Patchell, *The Palmerin Romances in Elizabethan Prose
Fiction* (New York, 1947); John J. O'Connor, *"Amadis de Gaule" and Its In-
fluence on Elizabethan Literature* (New Brunswick, N. J., 1970); and A. C.
Hamilton, "Sidney's *Arcadia* as Prose Fiction: Its Relation to Its Sources,"
ELR 2 (1972): 29-60. Hamilton notes that "in creating his fiction, Sidney

sought to make it comprehensive. Consequently, when he turned to continental models, he was committed to no one of them. Within one work, he made available for English writers the best in continental fiction: classical, medieval, and modern. His work displays the potentialities and limitations of each genre and the strength of their combination" (p. 33). This suggests that the *New Arcadia*, although within larger traditions, is more independent of its sources than its earlier critics had been willing to admit.

12. " 'The Countess of Pembroke's Arcadia,' " *The Second Common Reader* (New York, 1932; 1960), p. 40.

13. The   philosophic problems involved with the dyadic relationships are discussed at length by Ernst Cassirer in his *The Philosophy of Symbolic Forms*, trans. Ralph Manheim, 3 vols. (New Haven, 1953; 1968), 2: 83-151 and 3: 107-277.

2

Book I and the Structure of Space

i

Two critical truisms are that the *Arcadia* begins *in medias res* and that this contrasts it with the *Old Arcadia*. Kenneth O. Myrick uses the *in medias res* beginning to substantiate his theory that Sidney revised his work in light of the rules of heroic poetry as set down by Minturno and his remarks can stand for the consensus in this regard:

> In the *Old Arcadia* . . . Sidney begins with exposition, sketching first the circumstances which led to Basilius' retirement, and then the events which brought the two princes into Arcadia. In the revised version he plunges at once into the story, with the scene between Strephon and Claius, or, if we regard that scene as a kind of prologue, he begins with the arrival of Musidorus' half-drowned

body on the shore near where the shepherds are standing. Whichever view we take of the scene between Strephon and Claius, the *New Arcadia* plunges *in medias res*. The *Old Arcadia* begins *ab ovo*.[1]

There is little in these remarks by Myrick to which exception can be taken.[2] But they do not explain the effect of the *in medias res* beginning of the *Arcadia* nor do they account for the remarkable similarity between the first book of the *Old Arcadia* and its counterpart in the revised version.

Two interrelated effects of the choice of the *in medias res* beginning as a literary strategy are immediately obvious: chronological sequence in plot is deemphasized in favor of either a single crucial episode, as in most Greek tragedies, or in favor of thematic sequence, as in the *Arcadia*, so that the narrator is forced to delegate portions of the narrative to the characters. In the latter case in particular, the *in medias res* beginning precludes the exclusive use of the omniscient voice. Narration of past events demands the use of voice that is not omniscient and is usually satisfied by the internalized narration of one character to another in order to explain some present situation. If this kind of flashback technique is to be successful, the artist must carefully establish the dramatic need for it.[3] Carefully handled, as in the manner of Sidney, the delegated narrations may serve to provide motivation within the main narrative line or they may be used to provide suspense both forwards and backwards. "Not only is the reader concerned to know events as they *will* happen, but also the disposition of events as they *have* happened. Voice in the latter case modulates to the preterite and pluperfect tenses."[4] Characterization may be enhanced through the delegated narrations with the character-narrators revealing themselves in subtle ways. Simultaneously, the ironic possibilities built into the character-narrators' relative ignorance may be exploited by means of the delegated narrations. Finally, the use of delegated narrations involves a marked shift in the audience's sense of the narrator's omniscience, a shift that changes the audience's role in the narration.

In the *Old Arcadia*, when it becomes necessary to report past events, the narrator interposes himself between the audience and the events by making a radical and overt shift in the point of view. Thus, for example, when Pyrocles (in this version disguised as Cleophila), after gaining access to Basilius's retreat, seeks out Musidorus, he discovers his friend disguised as the shepherd Dorus and singing a love complaint. The narrator begins his explanation of the transformation by saying:

> And now having named him [Musidorus], methinks it reason I should tell you what chance brought him to this change. I left him lately, if you remember, fair ladies, in the grove. (*OA*, 40)

The interjection of the narrator pulls the audience out of the work, and reminds them that they are viewing the events, as it were, from above and alongside the omniscient narrator. The revision in the *New Arcadia* handles matters differently; at the corresponding point (I, 112ff.), Musidorus explains the change in himself. Information is thus restricted to the point of view operating at the moment and the audience is kept within the framework of the events as they occur or as they are reported by the participants. The possibility for empathy is, then, greater in the revised version than in the *Old Arcadia*. This does not mean, however, that there are no shifts of point of view in the *Arcadia*, for obviously there are; the opening chapter, with its shift of focus from Strephon and Claius to Musidorus, is a case in point. But the narrative shifts tend in the *Arcadia* to be internal[5] rather than external as they are in the original version. And this may provide a key to the function of the *in medias res* beginning of the *Arcadia*; it serves to internalize the audience into the fiction by changing the stance of the narrator.

The difference between narrative stances of the two *Arcadias* helps to explain an often-noticed tonal difference between the two works. Both works deal in a fundamental way with what Mark Rose calls "the morality of passionate love." In the older version, however, "greater weight is given to the humanist ethic of reason." The work "has relatively little to say about the virtues of love."[6] The exponent of the humanist ethic of reason in the *Old Arcadia* is the narrator; distanced from his characters, he "looks on approvingly, but also critically."[7] The rhetorical effect of this distancing might well be called mildly satiric comedy. The work is mildly satirical in the ethical correctives provided by the narrator and comic in the narrative, which ends happily in spite of the follies and excesses of all the central characters, Pyrocles and Musidorus included. The internalization of narrator and audience into the *Arcadia* requires a different handling of moral issues if the narrative is still to have a comic ending and if the work is to fulfill the didactic impulse that Sidney ascribes to poetry. Sidney copes with this problem by eliminating almost entirely the follies of the princes and by focusing our empathy on them. The retrospective narratives, then, have as part of their function the job of outlining the outer parameters of passionate love, both its excesses and its virtues.[8] Walter Davis's view that in the *Arcadia* passionate love ought not to be seen as a good, except insofar as it leads to divine love, is therefore more appropriate to the *Old Arcadia* than to the *Arcadia*.[9]

The second major effect of an *in medias res* beginning, in addition but related to the internalization of point of view, is the deemphasis of chronological plotting. This effect, however, is hardly evident in Book I of the *Arcadia*. In fact, a comparison of the two versions shows virtually no disruption of the chronology of the first book of the *Old Arcadia* in the revised version.[10] Basically the difference between the first books of the two versions consists of added incidents and two significant deletions.[11] Moreover, the order of the corresponding events is essentially the same in the two versions. The temporal sequence of the first book of the *Arcadia*, despite the *in medias res* beginning, is straightforward and on-going; there is little suggestion of the relationship between events in the present and those of the past or future beyond immediate context. Exceptions to this are brief and easily passed over,

such as Pyrocles' remark as to why he chose the name Zelmane
for his disguise: " 'Therefore in the closest manner I could,
naming myself Zelmane, for that dear lady's sake, to whose
memory I am so much bound, I caused this apparel to be
made . . .' " (I, 86). This enigmatic comment, however, remains unexplained until the second book of the *Arcadia* and
with this bare hint the possible significance of the past is
passed over.[12] Similarly, with the exception of the on-going
primary plot of the princes' loves, there is little looking forward in the first book. Although the characters introduced
in the three love-episodes of Book I — Argalus and Parthenia,
Helen and Amphialus, and Phalantus and Artesia — become
important in later portions of the story, the episodes in
which they appear in Book I seem, with the notable exception
of the Helen-Amphialus relationship, to be terminal. Parthenia
and Argalus are happily married after the successful conclusion of the Helots' rebellion and after Parthenia's magical
cure at the hands of Helen. Phalantus's quest and false love
for Artesia is ended by Pyrocles' victory at the joust. Only
Helen's love for Amphialus and the love triangle between
Strephon, Claius, and Urania are left unresolved.[13] The lack
of emphasis on temporal matters suggested here is a corollary
to what will be seen as Book I's stress on spatial relationships.

ii

The *Arcadia* opens not with the introduction of Pyrocles
and Musidorus but with the complaints of the young shepherds, Strephon and Claius, who lament the loss of their
beloved, Urania. These two pastoral characters are of minimal importance to the plot of Sidney's work, for they exist
solely to aid Musidorus in his attempted rescue of Pyrocles
and to escort him to the safety of Kalander's house. They
disappear from all but the eclogues after the second chapter,[14]
and Urania never appears on the scene at all. Her departure
from Arcadia is mourned in the opening passages of the

Arcadia; a letter written by her calls Strephon and Claius away from Kalander's house (I, 15); and her portrait is among those of the conquered beauties in Phalantus's tournament (I, 104). What, then, is to be made of this curious opening? Myrick suggests that it is to serve as an invocation in accordance with the rules for epic poetry as laid down by Minturno.[15] But the view of the opening as an invocation accepts it as not tied closely to the plot of the *Arcadia* and only in a most general sense thematically related to the rest of the work; therefore an explanation that relates more integrally the opening to the work is to be preferred. Moreover, Katherine Duncan-Jones objects quite rightly to Myrick's claim that ". . . the praise [of Urania] is couched in just the mood of reverent adoration appropriate to the poet's prayer to his Muse."[16] She notes that Myrick fails to mention the fact that the praise of Urania occurs in a "complaint for a departed Muse . . . [rather than in] a hopeful address to a present one."[17] Similarly, even if the interpretations that allegorically identify Urania as either the Countess of Pembroke[18] or Queen Elizabeth[19] are accepted, they are not of much assistance to a reading of the *Arcadia* as other than a historical allegory.[20] Finally, while the incomplete state of the *New Arcadia* does not preclude the possibility that Sidney fully intended to bring Urania and her two lovers back into the action at some later point, the opening passage ought at least to be thematically connected in some specific way to the rest of the work as it now stands.

In recent years two scholars, Walter R. Davis and Mark Rose, have attempted to find specific thematic connections between the complaints of Strephon and Claius and the rest of the *Arcadia*. Davis sees Urania as symbolizing Heavenly Love and associates her with Aphrodite Ourania. Thus, he claims, having initiated the process of love in the shepherds, she leaves them bereaved but prepared to climb to the higher orders of love by themselves. Davis then goes on to argue that this is emblematic of "the possible transformations of the soul that love holds out to all men."[21] Urania serves to ini-

tiate the audience along with Strephon and Claius into the
mysteries of Neoplatonic love, the nature of which, Davis
contends, is set down in Claius's consolation:

> No, no, let us think with consideration, and consider with acknow-
> ledging, and acknowledge with admiration, and admire with love,
> and love with joy in the midst of all woes: let us in such sort think,
> I say, that our poor eyes were so enriched as to behold, and our low
> hearts so exalted as to love, a maid, who is such, that as the greatest
> thing the world can show, is her beauty, so the least thing that
> may be praised in her, is her beauty . . . hath not the only love
> of her made us (being silly ignorant shepherds) raise up our
> thoughts above the ordinary level of the world, so as great clerks do
> not disdain our conference? Hath not the desire to seem worthy in
> her eyes made us when others were sleeping, to sit viewing the course
> of heavens? When others were running at Base, to run over learned
> writings? When others mark their sheep, we to mark ourselves? Hath
> not she thrown reason upon our desires, and, as it were, given eyes
> unto Cupid? Hath in any, but in her, love-fellowship maintained
> friendship between rivals, and beauty taught the beholders chas-
> tity? (I, 7-8)

Davis argues that this passage presents in outline form the
Neoplatonic ladder of love. Under Urania's tutelage Strephon
and Claius have progressed from delight in corporeal beauty
to delight in the virtues of the body images. After Urania left,
Davis goes on to say, they moved from moral to metaphysical
values "and 'traced the footsteps of God' in the created universe, thereby perceiving their essential harmony with the emblematic universe of divine order around them."[22] This way
of looking at Urania is, of course, in keeping with Davis's
thematic reading of the entire *Arcadia*, for he sees in Sidney's
work a presentation of Pyrocles and Musidorus climbing the
ladder of love.

There are, unfortunately, two difficulties with this interpretation. On the one hand, the Neoplatonic reading of the
Arcadia is suspect and, on the other, Davis's reading of this
passage neglects the immediate context of the dialogue between Strephon and Claius. The second difficulty is especially

to the point here. Strephon's complaint opens the exchange and it is not in the key of Neoplatonic aspiration toward completion but in anguish.

> "O my Claius," said he, "hither we are now come to pay the rent, for which we are so called unto by over-busy Remembrance, Remembrance, restless Remembrance, which claims not only this duty of us, but for it will have us forget ourselves." (I, 5)

Surely this is not the cry of one who has perceived the "essential harmony . . . of divine order." The last clause, ". . . it will have us forget ourselves," stands in marked contrast to the inference that Davis draws from Claius's remark that we "mark ourselves." The final lines of Strephon's complaint, moreover, stress what he and Claius have lost rather than what they have supposedly gained:

> "But woe is me, yonder, yonder, did she put her foot into the boat, at that instant as it were dividing her heavenly beauty, between the earth and the sea. But when she was embarked, did you not mark how the winds whistled, and the seas danced for joy, how the sails did swell with pride, and all because they had Urania? O Urania, blessed be thou Urania, the sweetest fairness and the fairest sweetness!"
>   With that word his voice broke so with sobbing, that he could say no further. (I, 6)

Claius's response to Strephon's lament begins: " 'Alas my Strephon,' said he, 'what needs this score to reckon up only our losses?' " (I, 6-7) and moves into the praise of love and of Urania cited above. His speech, offered in the spirit of consolation, ought to be read in conjunction with Strephon's lament and not be taken independently as the underlying doctrine of Sidney's *Arcadia*. This undercuts the claim for Urania as simply the symbol of "Heavenly Love." Moreover, the effect of Urania on Strephon and Claius must be assessed in terms of both of them so that their differing reactions to her absence points to different facets of love's power. The polar vision of love — love as both loss and gain — is charac-

teristic of the *Arcadia* and precludes a simplistic interpretation, no matter how erudite, of love's force in the work.[23]

Urania is seen differently by Mark Rose who, incidentally,
rejects Davis's overall thesis as well. Like Davis, Rose notes
that Urania's name recalls "both the muse Urania, patron of
divine contemplation, and Venus Urania, patron of heavenly
love."[24] But where Davis stresses the symbolic aspect of
Urania, Rose stresses her actual divinity. Her presence makes
Arcadia the ideal state in which love can flourish and her
departure has the same effect on that state as did the fall of
Adam and Eve — the introduction of imperfection into the
affairs of men. Thus Rose argues that the departure of Urania
is a symbolic fall into the world of our own experience and
that "Arcadia aspires . . . to regain the ordered serenity of the
pastoral ideal, to find some satisfactory substitute for Venus
Urania."[25] This reading, though attractive, suffers from an
overemphasis on Urania's supposed divinity. Rose neglects
the presence of Urania's picture among those of the other
conquered beauties of Phalantus's tourney because to see
Urania as primarily a divine figure results in a disquieting dis-
crepancy between levels of presentation during Phalantus's
tourney. There is much to be said, therefore, for Miss Duncan-
Jones's complaint that "Venus Urania, whom Ficino describes
as begotten of the Angelic mind, seems altogether too large a
conception to be fused with the simple shepherdess shown
in the portrait defended by Lalus."[26]

A way out of this morass seems both desirable and possible.
The assumption implicit in earlier criticism is that Urania's
name is to be taken according to some sort of identification
function, that Urania — the character in Sidney's work — is
to be identified with either Urania — the muse of divine contemplation — or Venus Urania — patron of heavenly love. If,
however, the relationship between Urania's name and those
of the mythological characters is one of association rather
than one of identification, the problem of "discrepancies
between levels of presentation" may be circumvented and
Urania may be understood simultaneously as the purely

human love-object of Strephon and Claius and as a symbol for something outside herself.[27] That something must be, of course, the force of love itself. Moreover, the force of love associated with Urania is also quite clearly associated with Arcadia and may be regarded as a *genius loci*. With Urania's withdrawal the land is transformed in the minds of her shepherd lovers. This is evident in the double sestina of their composition, "Ye Goatherd Gods," which Lamon sings in "The First Eclogues," the conclusion of which follows:

Strephon.   For she whose parts maintain'd a perfect music
            Whose beauty shin'd more than the blushing morning,
            Who much did pass in state the stately mountains,
            In straightness pass'd the cedars of the forests,
            Hath cast me wretch into eternal evening,
            By taking her two suns from these dark valleys.

Klaius.   For she, to whom compar'd, the Alps are valleys,
            She, whose least word brings from the spheres their music,
            At whose approach the sun rose in the evening,
            Who where she went bare in her forehead morning,
            Is gone, is gone, from these our spoiled forests,
            Turning to deserts our best pastur'd mountains.

Strephon.   These mountains witness shall, so shall these valleys,

Klaius.   These forests eke, made wretched by our music,
            Our morning hymn is this, and song at evening.
                               (I, 142-43)

Clearly, in the minds of Strephon and Claius the very appearance of Arcadia is directly tied to their relationship with Urania. The landscape is turned by their grief from "grassy mountains" and "pleasant valleys" to "spoiled forests" and "deserts." In fact, as David Kalstone, speaking of the whole double sestina, points out, "As the poem progresses . . . elements of landscape take their places metaphorically as part of the inner world of fancy and lose their status as solid objects."[28] Urania's symbolic function, then, shows the power of love in spatial terms — the elements of landscape in the inner fancy — and shows how a psychological state influences one's perception of space.

iii

Just as Arcadia is transformed into a wasteland in the minds of Claius and Strephon after the departure of Urania, it is changed into a demi-paradise in Pyrocles' mind after he falls in love with Philoclea.

> "And lord, dear cousin," said he, "doth not the pleasantness of this place carry in itself sufficient reward for any time lost in it? Do you not see how all things conspire together to make this country a heavenly dwelling?" (I, 57)

Pyrocles goes on to catalogue the diverse beauties of Arcadia, concluding that ". . . it must needs be that some goddess inhabiteth this region, who is the soul of this soil . . . " (I, 57). Musidorus in his reply is willing to grant that Arcadia is a pleasant enough place, but no more so than either Pyrocles' home country, Macedon, or Musidorus's Thessalia. He then goes on to argue that Pyrocles' description of Arcadia is more a product of his friend's mind than the actuality of the countryside. Musidorus, at this point, has not experienced the transformation that love has wrought in Pyrocles, so his vision is uncolored by emotional response. But this does not mean that his view has greater validity than that of his friend, for Book I suggests strongly that one's sense of the way things are is at least partially determined by who one is and by the situation in which one finds himself. Moreover, since what is outside the self is open only to perception, reality is a construct built by the interaction of self and non-self, of mind (which includes the emotions, the sense of moral hierarchies, and so forth) and all things outside the mind. Within limits, things are as we perceive them to be; conversely, descriptions are as much about the perceiver as about the thing perceived. Musidorus is no more right than

Pyrocles; here, as elsewhere in Book I, spatial descriptions
are maps of psychological and social states as well as orna-
ments to be enjoyed as such. They serve to organize the
thematic material. If the mind is overly stressed in this interaction between
mind and world, the result is some sort of ethical and aes-
thetic relativism. But Sidney is careful to grant the world
its due and to show how visual effect affects psychological
response. The description of the castaway Musidorus (I, 8-9),
for example, which interrupts the meditations of Claius and
Strephon, makes extensive use of verbs of sight and of visual
images, which gives it a static, tapestrylike effect. The reader
discovers the scene seen by Strephon and Claius, he feels
their suspense, and he reacts with them in their attempt to
save Musidorus. What is important here is not so much that
Strephon and Claius react to events in the outside world but
that the static quality of the description makes it seem as if
they are reacting to a painting, not to reality itself. The
pattern of this sequence thus parallels the pattern of the be-
ginnings of Pyrocles' love for Philoclea: he sees her portrait
at Kalander's house, falls in love, and disguises himself in
order to join with her in the Arcadian retreat. The beginning
of Musidorus's love of Pamela follows an identical pattern
with one significant difference: what he sees is not a picture
of Pamela but the girl herself. In each of these sequences, the
participants undergo significant psychological change as a
result of what they perceive. In each, the world acts on them
and they change their ways of seeing it. Consequently, the
world itself changes. Finally we should notice that the
three sequences begin slightly differently: Strephon and
Claius see a scene that is presented with pictorial qualities,
Pyrocles sees a picture, and Musidorus sees Pamela herself.
This should suggest that, for Sidney, painting is a means of
organizing raw experience but is not significantly different
from experience itself. Since painting is a spatial art, it is
not surprising to find that the experiences in Book I are
presented in language that shares qualities with painting.

In addition to showing the interrelationship between self and world, the descriptive passages of the first book also serve to modulate rhetorically the reader's response. After Musidorus has been restrained from his suicide attempt, for example, he insists on making an attempt to rescue Pyrocles. Strephon and Claius aid him in borrowing a boat from a fisherman and they set forth,

> and were no sooner gone beyond the mouth of the haven, but that some way into the sea they might discern (as it were) a stain of the water's color, and betimes some sparks and smoke mounting thereout. But the young man no sooner saw it, but that beating his breast, he cried, that there was the beginning of his ruin, entreating them to bend their course as near unto it as they could: telling, how they smoke was but a small relic of a great fire, which had driven both him and his friend rather to commit themselves to the cold mercy of the sea, than to abide the hot cruelty of the fire: and that therefore, though they both had abandoned the ship, that he was (if anywhere) in that course to be met withal. They steered therefore as near thitherward as they could: but when they came so near as their eyes were full masters of the object, they saw a sight full of piteous strangeness:a ship, or rather the carcass of the ship, or rather some few bones of the carcass, hulling there, part broken, part burned, part drowned: death having used more than one dart to that destruction. About it floated great store of very rich things, and many chests which might promise no less. And amidst the precious things were a number of dead bodies, which likewise did not only testify both elements' violence, but that the chief violence was grown of human inhumanity: for their bodies were full of grisly wounds, and their blood had (as it were) filled the wrinkles of the sea's visage: which it seemed the sea would not wash away, that it might witness it is not always his fault, when we condemn his cruelty. In sum, a defeat where the conquered kept both field and spoil: a shipwreck without storm or fill-footing: and a waste of fire in the midst of the water. (I, 9-10)

This description moves through increasingly destructive circles until it reaches a vortex in the final evaluative comments concerning the waste of violence. From the destroyed ship, to the lost wealth, to the mutilated corpses the passage proceeds with increasing horror, which is heightened by unnatural juxtapositions — the dead men, who should return to dust, out of their element but surrounded by the ruins of their earthly aspirations of wealth, and the fire on the water. But this panorama of death and destruction does not stand in isolation and E.M.W. Tillyard is surely right when he says of the *Arcadia*, ". . . it begins with a contrast, both of substance and style, between the idea of man's 'erected wit' and the pitiful spectacle of what in crude fact man has made of man."[29] The contrast between the pastoral elegy of Strephon and Claius and this description of the remains of human conflict serves as a shocking notice to the audience that the world of the *Arcadia* is not the ideal world either of innocence, which is free from the violence of human strife, or of heroism, in which the gore of the battlefield is seen as a good. As with the problem of love's force, the reader is warned away from a simplistic or absolutist interpretation of the balance between the idyllic and the heroic, and the contrast serves as that warning.

The description of the shipwreck has yet another function: it holds knowledge of Pyrocles' fate in abeyance in order to increase suspense. Musidorus and the fishermen find Pyrocles riding a piece of the mast and prepare to throw him a rope. But the fishermen are so awed by the sight of the young man waving his sword about his head that they mistake him for "some god begotten between Neptune and Venus, that had made all this terrible slaughter' (I, 10), and sail by without rescuing him. Before they can return, Pyrocles is captured by some pirates and separated once again from Musidorus. Throughout this description, the sense of visual image overrides the sense of action; what is seen seems more important than what is done.

The opening debate between Strephon and Claius and the events that follow it are all presented as if in stasis, "figured forth," as it were. Feelings and events are spots in place rather than movements. A number of effects follow from this. The static qualities allow for a style that focuses on the interrelationship between perception and the world here to show that man creates the world in which he lives according to the way he sees it. The creative act is not solipsistic, however, but arises out of interaction with things and events outside the self. In the *Apology*, Sidney claims that " . . . the skill of ech Artificer standeth in that *Idea* or fore conceit of the worke, and not in the worke it selfe. And that the Poet hath that *Idea*, is manifest, by delivering them foorth in such excellencie as he had imagined them: which delivering foorth, also is not wholly imaginative . . . " (III, 8). Although Sidney is talking about artistic creation here, not ordinary perception, it is clear that the way characters see the world in Book I of the *Arcadia* is analogous to his theory of artistic creation. The shock of this analogy may be reduced when we remember that God, "having made man to his owne likenes, set him beyond and over all the workes of that second nature, which in nothing he sheweth so much as in poetry . . . " (III, 8). Poetry is just the special case of human nature and the impulse shared by the characters of the *Arcadia* to shape the world is an impulse common to all men. If this is granted, it follows that the test of such visionary activities lies, as Sidney claims in the *Apology*, in the "fore conceit" that underlies them. Thus, for example, acceptance of "goodness" of Pyrocles' love for Philoclea leads necessarily to an acceptance of his vision of the Arcadian state, while acceptance of Musidorus's opposition to love leads to a rejection of Pyrocles' position. Matters are complicated, however, by degrees of idealism. As characters become more idealistic, they allow the world its due less and the world becomes more impervious to their visions. The failures of such solipsistic idealism may provide the basis for the problem of the characters in Helen of Corinth's story later in Book I and may suggest a way of looking at Phalantus's fashionable love of Artesia near the close of the book. Finally, we should notice that the rhetorical effect of the spatial descriptions is educative. Not only does it delight us but it reminds us that, like the characters in the *Arcadia*, we organize our perceptions according to preconceived notions of how the world is; since the world of the book is part of the perceived world, the same tests apply to our vision of Sidney's work as to the visions of the characters within the work.

The spatial descriptions in the first chapter of Book I may be said to center on the interrelationship of the individual and the world; those of the second chapter center on the interrelationship between society and the world. This is particularly evident in the contrast noticed by Musidorus between Laconia and Arcadia. Relieved to know that Pyrocles has not been killed in the shipwreck that brought him to the shores of Laconia, Musidorus allows Strephon and Claius to take him to "a gentleman, by name Kalander, who vouchsafest much favor unto us" (I, 12). The first two days of the journey are through the barren lands of Laconia. On the third day, Arcadia

> welcomed Musidorus' eyes (wearied with the wasted soil of Laconia) with delightful prospects. There were hills which garnished their proud heights with stately trees: humble valleys, whose base estate seemed comforted with refreshing of silver rivers: meadows, enamelled with all sorts of eye-pleasing flowers: thickets, which being lined with most pleasant shade, were witnessed so to by the cheerful disposition of many well-tuned birds: each pasture stored with sheep feeding with sober security, while the pretty lambs with bleating oratory craved the dams' comfort: here a shepherd's boy piping, as though he should never be old: there a young shepherdess knitting, and withal singing, and it seemed that her voice comforted her hands to work, and her hands kept time to her voice's music. As for the houses of the country (for many houses came under their eye) they were all scattered, no two being one by the other, and yet not so far off as that it barred mutual succor: a show, as it were, of an accompanable solitariness, and of a civil wildness. (I, 13-14)

More than a contrast between "the wasted soil of Laconia" and the "delightful prospects" of Arcadia, this passage suggests a number of things about both Arcadia and Sidney's arcadian style. Hazlitt, using this passage as an example, attacks Sidney's prose style for its "unceasing craving after intellectual excitement."

He must officiously and gratuitously interpose between you and the subject as the cicerone of Nature, distracting the eye and the mind by continual uncalled-for interruptions, analysing, dissecting, dis-jointing, murdering everything, and reading a pragmatical, self-sufficient lecture over the dead body of nature.[30]

Although Hazlitt's diatribe is perhaps more an appraisal of his own sensibility than of Sidney's style, he touches on an important aspect of Sidney's work. Superficial impressions of floridity notwithstanding, Sidney's prose tends to be analytic in a way that reveals the complexity of problems rather than their simplicity. For example, the two illustrations of *synoeciosis* (composition by contraries) in the final clause of Sidney's description of Arcadia, "accompanable solitariness" and "civil wildness," clearly point to a need for a proper balance between nature and what might be called the forces of civilization in Arcadia.

A failure to recognize the presence of complexity and the need for balance in passages such as this can lead to overstressing of primitivism in the Arcadian state. Ernest S. Gohn is probably quite right to suggest that the virtues of Arcadia are not restricted to the old classic virtues of temperance and moderation although they are among the Arcadian virtues. But Gohn goes too far in his acceptance of the serene life of following nature with a well-tempered mind and he overstates his case when he says, "The impression of the desirability of such a simple life is strengthened by the fact that Sidney always speaks of Arcadia in such idyllic terms."[31] To overstress the pastoral element leads necessarily to a problem of interpretation: "The difficulty is that Sidney has two opposing ethical standards [heroic and primitivistic[32]] which do not coalesce."[33] This implies a conflict of interest on Sidney's part between a desire to show men the ways of virtuous action and a yearning for a past when life was less complex. But the two standards do in fact complement each other. It is through heroic action under the dictates of right reason that the idyllic state is created and maintained. The results of Basilius's retreat so clearly show that withdrawal from the complexities of the social and political organism can be a direct cause in the decline of the ideal state.

Musidorus is startled, as are we, to find contiguous states "so diverse in show, the one wanting no store, th'other having no store but of want" (I, 14), but Claius explains that the desolation of Laconia is not natural in origins but social and political. Laconia is "not so poor by the barrenness of the soil (though in itself not passing fertile) as by a civil war, which . . . hath in this sort as it were disfigured the face of nature . . . " (I, 14). The metaphor Claius chooses to describe the effects of the Helots' revolt on Laconia, "disfigured the face of nature," is in accord with the language of space used so often in Book I and suggests the fundamental interaction between social order and landscape. The "delightful prospects" of Arcadia, Claius goes on to say, result from the fact that its population is "a happy people, wanting little, because they desire not much" (I, 14). The political implications of Claius's claim of the "happy people" of Arcadia are apparent as soon as we recall that such happiness is possible only in a country that is governed well and politically stable. Yet we may also notice that Claius's claim that the people of Arcadia "desire not much" ties the political stability of the land — soon to be disrupted because of Basilius's retreat — to the individual visions of each of the shepherds. In this way, the kind of individual orientation seen in the first chapter is tied to the social orientation seen in the second chapter.

Kalander takes up these interrelationships between the individual, the society, and the physical environment in his explanation to Musidorus of the situation in Arcadia:

> This country Arcadia among all the provinces of Greece, hath ever been had in singular reputation: partly for the sweetness of the air, and other natural benefits, but principally for the well-tempered minds of the people. (I, 19)

The fact that the Arcadian populace is characterized by "well-tempered minds," Kalander goes on to claim, has not only prevented the sort of civil strife that laid waste to Laconia but has also inhibited conflict between Arcadia and her neighbors. Because Arcadia is so peaceful a country, even the Muses have honored it "by choosing this country for their chief repairing place" (I, 19) and by granting the shepherds of the land the gift of poetry. Arcadia's ruler is Basilius, who, as Kalander explains, is "a prince of sufficient skill to govern so quiet a country, where the good minds of the former princes had set down good laws" (I, 19). Basilius,

> though he exceed not in the virtues which get admiration; as depth of wisdom, height of courage and largeness of magnificence, yet is he notable in those which stir affection, as truth of word, meekness, courtesy, mercifulness, and liberality. (I, 19)

Although his virtues are not of the kind that would enable Basilius to found an idyllic state, they have enabled him to maintain it in the past. But Basilius has chosen, for reasons made clear much later in the *Arcadia*, to go into retreat with his family against the advice of his best counsellor, Philanax, to "let your subjects have you in their eyes; let them see the benefits of your justice daily more and more; and so must they needs rather like of present sureties, than uncertain changes" (I, 25). The effects of Basilius's ill-advised retreat begin manifesting themselves almost immediately. His withdrawal creates consternation in the people, "among whom many strange bruits are received for current, and with some appearance of danger in respect of the valiant Amphialus" (I, 26), Basilius's nephew. The nobles are discontented, Kalander reports, and envious of the advancement of the virtuous Philanax who was appointed viceregent. Clearly, then, the idyllic life enjoyed in Arcadia is not, strictly speaking, a natural state. Overt action is necessary for its preservation; such passivity as is tied to the course taken by Basilius invites the forces that are under control in the ideal state to run amuck.

The opening chapters of the *Arcadia*, then, introduce the two thematic threads that will run intermingled throughout the rest of the work. The first of these may be called the erotic theme[34] and the second, the political or social theme.[35] Each theme, moreover, is so presented as to show how erotic and political entanglements structure space. The events that follow hard on the heels of Musidorus's return to health show how the two motifs are in fact not separate, but interrelated. The love between Argalus and Parthenia and the revolt of the Helots are so closely tied that the two themes are inseparable. And the sequence, with its successful resolution on both the erotic and the political planes, may serve as an emblem of the whole *Arcadia*. Just as the affairs of the princes are interrupted by Cecropia's rebellion, the Helots' revolt is part of the interlude of the love of Argalus and Parthenia; and just as Basilius foolishly tries to prevent his daughters' marriages, Parthenia's mother willfully tries to force her daughter to accept the ignoble Demagoras. These developments in the narrative will be clarified in what follows.

iv

Settled comfortably in Kalander's household, Musidorus is surprised by his host's sudden withdrawal one evening before dinner and bemused by his continued absence during the following days. He presses the steward for the reason and hears from him the story of the Argalus-Parthenia-Demagoras triangle and its effects on the Helots' revolt. There are several significant features to the steward's story. In terms of the relationship between Pyrocles and Musidorus, it is important to note that friendship, "which is so rare, as it is to be doubted whether it be a thing in deed, or but a word" (I, 32), motivates Clitophon's attempted rescue of Argalus. Likewise it is important to see that it is Demagoras's failure in the

erotic sphere that advances the Helots' political cause, for
Parthenia's rejection leads directly to his captainship of the
Helots. The intertwining of the two motifs is also evident in
that Argalus's faithful love of Parthenia leads him to his
revenge on Demagoras: the vacancy thus left will be filled by
Pyrocles, who brings the Helots' revolt to a satisfactory conclusion. But perhaps most significant of all is the effect of
the erotic drive on the physical appearance of Parthenia.
Demagoras is unable to look below the surface and sees only
her outward appearance, which is for him the sole reality. The
attraction that she has for Demagoras is established to be lust,
for Demagoras is "a man mighty in riches and power, and
proud thereof, stubbornly stout, loving nobody but himself,
and for his own delight's sake Parthenia" (I, 32). It is not
surprising, then, that Demagoras tries to destroy Parthenia's
beauty, which is the source of his pleasure in her, when he
sees that his suit is doomed. Both out of the frustration of
his own desires and, even more, out of the envy at Argalus's
success with Parthenia, Demagoras "rubbed all over her face
a most horrible poison: the effect whereof was such, that
never leper looked more ugly than she did . . . " (I, 34).

But it would be a misattribution to place all the responsibility for Demagoras's lust on Parthenia's beauty; had he not
been a man "loving nobody but himself" it is unlikely that
his response to Parthenia's perfections would have been lustful. In fact, it might be said that his lust makes Parthenia's
features ugly in much the same way that his poison does.
This, of course, is in marked contrast to the way that Argalus's
love beautifies Parthenia even after Demagoras's revenge.
Although "with the most abundant kindness that an eye-
ravished lover can express, he [Argalus] labored both to
drive the extremity of sorrow from her, and to hasten the
celebration of their marriage" (I, 35), Parthenia "could not
find in her heart he should be tied to what was unworthy of
his presence" (I, 35). Argalus's reasons for behaving like an
"eye-ravished lover" indicate that for him Parthenia's beauty
is at least as much the product of his love as it is the cause of

it, for, in attempting to persuade Parthenia to go ahead with the marriage in spite of the disfigurement, he

> conjured her by remembrance of her affection, and true oaths of his own affection, not to make him so unhappy, as to think he had not only lost her face, but her heart; that her face, when it was fairest, had been but as a marshall, to lodge the love of her in his mind; which now was so well placed, as it needed no further help of any outward harbinger. (I, 35)

Argalus goes on to argue that, despite the outward effects of the poison, Parthenia remains beautiful to him because of their love: her injured skin "to him was most fair, since it was hers . . . " (I, 35) and "he never beheld it, but therein he saw the loveliness of her love toward him . . . " (I, 36). It is not enough to say, then, that Argalus continues to love Parthenia for what she is rather than for her beauty; to him she is still beautiful. His perception of her is governed by his attitudes toward her; his love could, if Parthenia would let it, serve as a partial antidote to Demagoras's poison.

Set against the erotic component stressed in the steward's story of Clitophon, Argalus, and Parthenia is the political component stressed in Musidorus's preparations for the rescue of Clitophon and Argalus. Seeing at once the raggle-taggle quality of the forces gathered by Kalander, Musidorus immediately takes effective command and attempts to discover the nature of the forces he is to attack. What he discovers is that the Helots had been in the past freemen and landholders but that under the rule of the Lacedaemonians they had been deprived of both property and freedom. Resentful of Lacedaemonian tyranny, the Helots have rebelled against their oppresors and, under the captainship of Pyrocles, who took over after the death of the wanton and bloody Demagoras, have gained some measure of success. Irving Ribner notes that both Sidney and Machiavelli, to whom Ribner argues Sidney was indebted at least to the degree that he was borrowing from a tradition of political commonplaces of which the

Florentine is the high mark, "would have condemned the methods used by the Lacedemonians."[36] Whether or not Machiavellianism is an appropriate label for Sidney's politics, the reign of the Lacedaemonians is one of misrule and one that could not have been better calculated to ferment a revolt. And while it would be difficult to determine from Sidney's handling of the Helots' revolt his attitudes toward rebellion, it is evident that oppression is not, in the *Arcadia* at least, included among viable forms of rule. Moreover, the differing results gained by the Helots under Demagoras and under Pyrocles indicate the place of reason in politics. Pyrocles had subdued their blood fury, persuaded them to act more moderately, and been an effective military leader. While Demagoras had led the Helots, the Lacedaemonians had been afraid to parley, but seeing the effectiveness of Pyrocles' command " . . . the estate of Lacedaemon had sent unto them [the Helots] , offering peace with most reasonable and honorable conditions" (I, 39). The peace offered to the Helots under Pyrocles contrasts with the terror and resistance offered them under Demagoras and so consists of a political goal to be sought.

Both the strategy by which the force under Musidorus enters the Helots' town and the reasons offered by Pyrocles for stopping the battle demonstrate the art of war as a political tool. In each instance, fighting is seen to be a means of achieving a particular real goal, not as a source of martial glory although martial glory may be a by-product and cowardice is certainly not condoned. The result of this attitude toward warfare is the weighing of possible losses against possible gains before initiating any combat. The clearest example of this is perhaps Pyrocles' recommendation that the Helots give up Kalander and Clitophon in preference to further conflict with the Arcadians:

"For first," said he, "since the strife is within our own home, if you lose, you lose all that in this life can be dear unto you: if you win, it will be a bloody victory with no profit, but the flattering in ourselves that same bad humor of revenge. Besides, it is like to stir Arcadia upon us, which now, by using these persons well, may be brought to some amity. Lastly, but especially, lest the king and nobility of Laconia (with whom now we have made a perfect peace) should hope by occasion of this quarrel to join the Arcadians with them, and so break off the profitable agreement already concluded. In sum, as in all deliberations (weighing the profit of the good success with the harm of the evil success) you shall find this way most safe and honorable." (I, 44)

And when fighting is chosen as the appropriate option, strategy like Musidorus's is a means of minimizing losses; Musidorus's venture against the Helots is finally more successful than the mission of Clitophon. The importance of "weighing the profit of the good success with the harm of the evil success" is that it argues the role of reason in military ventures, which are, after all, political tools.

The history of the Helots' revolt and of the conflict that finally settles it implies that the social and personal drives behind political action must be balanced by reason. This is shown through both positive and negative *exampla*. The unreasonable rule of the Lacedaemonians leads directly to the rebellion; and the unreasonable way the rebellion proceeds under Demagoras precludes the possibility of an honorable peace. The obviously carefully thought-out refusal of Philanax to involve his country in a civil war enables Pyrocles to make peace between the Helots and the Lacedaemonians,[37] a peace that corrects the earlier misrule by unifying the contesting parties. Thus the central article in the peace treaty is probably the one in which "the distinction of names between Helots and Lacedaemonians to be quite taken away, and all indifferently to enjoy both names and privileges of Laconians . . . and so you . . . to be hereafter fellows, and no longer servants" (I, 47). The importance granted to reason in these affairs does not, however, obviate personal and social drives. Rejection of oppression at least partially justifies the Helots' rebellion and

Clitophon's reason for his rescue attempt is surely admirable. Argalus's revenge on Demagoras is sufficiently prompted by the horrible nature of Demagoras's crime, but the suicidal nature of the assassination itself is suspect. It is apparently justified by the fact that, so far as he or the audience knows, Argalus's reason for living will be completed with the revenge. But this assumption is based on ignorance and is faulty, for Parthenia is being cured by Helen of Corinth's physician and will shortly return to Arcadia.

It is fitting that the Helot sequence does not underplay the role of emotions in political affairs, since it is the first sequence that mingles the erotic and political motifs. Just as the sequence begins with the love of Argalus and Parthenia, it ends with the successful conclusion of their story so that their love provides a frame for the political events. The peace that Pyrocles establishes between the Helots and the Lacedaemonians enables him to free Argalus, and no sooner do they arrive in Arcadia than they are joined by "a young noble lady, near kinswoman to the fair Helen Queen of Corinth" (I, 48), who bears an exceeding likeness to Parthenia. This young lady tells Argalus how Parthenia died from "the inward sore of her mind" (I, 49) and that she "before her death earnestly desiring, and persuading me, to think of no husband but of you; as of the only man in the world worthy to be loved . . ." (I, 49). The way Argalus refuses this legacy pleases Parthenia — for the young lady is indeed Parthenia — and demonstrates how completely his love controls his sense of his loved one: "it was Parthenia's self I loved, and love; which no likeness can make one; no commandment dissolve, no foulness defile, nor no death finish" (I, 50). This resurrection, as it were, of Parthenia is, then, the product of Argulus's fidelity. Since Parthenia tempts him in this way, we may infer that he would have lost her forever if he had accepted the offer of the "near kinswoman to the fair Helen" and failed "this trial, whether he would quickly forget his true Parthenia, or no" (I, 50). His success, however, leads to his marriage to his beloved and their marriage, after all their trials and tribulations, parallels the marriages that culminate the princes' stay in Arcadia.

v

It is perhaps typical of the way Sidney constructs his narrative that the Helot episode should be so multifunctional. Not only does it tie the thematic threads together in the manner of the *Arcadia* as a whole, but it also acts as preparation for Pyrocles' love-melancholy, which follows immediately, and for Musidorus's early indifference to love. The first signal of these developments in the narrative occurs even before the wedding takes place:

> Daiphantus marking her [Parthenia], "O Jupiter," said he speaking to Palladius, "how happens it, that beauty is only confined to Arcadia?"
> But Palladius not greatly attending his speech, some days were continued in the solemnizing the marriage, with all conceits that might deliver delight to men's fancies. (I, 54)

Pyrocles makes this remark because he has already seen the portrait of Philoclea in Kalander's garden and has fallen in love with her. Musidorus fails to understand the remark because he has yet to see Pamela and is not predisposed to love. The difference between the two heroes' states of mind established here creates the conflict that follows. But more important than such obvious interconnections between narrative sequences is the fact that the story of Argalus and Parthenia is an emblem of true love. As such it rhetorically prepares the audience to accept and admire Pyrocles' love for Philoclea by demonstrating the virtues of love; it inculcates in Pyrocles those virtues and so reduces any resistance he might otherwise have had to Philoclea's portrait. The same sort of juxtaposition of emblem and attitude can be found in the story Helen of Corinth tells Musidorus, which is followed by his violent attack on love.

When Pyrocles leaves the company of Kalander and Musidorus because "violence of love leads me into such a course, whereof your knowledge may much more vex you, than help me" (I, 61), Musidorus and Clitophon go in search of him. Discovering the abandoned armor of Amphialus, Musidorus dons it only to be assaulted by Helen of Corinth's retinue, who mistake him for Amphialus. After successfully defending himself and explaining how he came by the armor, Musidorus persuades Helen to tell her story. She explains that Amphialus was pressed into a surrogate's role for his friend Philoxenus and she fell in love with the intercessor. Philoxenus, discovering where Helen's affections rested, challenged Amphialus to a duel and, although Amphialus tried to avoid it, was killed. Grieved at the death of his friend and ashamed of his role in it, Amphialus "threw away his armor . . . and then (as ashamed of the light) he ran into [the] thickest of the woods, lamenting and . . . crying out . . . pitifully" (I, 71) and sending word back to Helen that " . . . I [Helen] was the cause of all this mischief: and that if I were a man, he would go over the world to kill me: but bade me assure myself, that of all creatures in the world, he most hated me" (I, 72). Unlike those in the story of Argalus and Parthenia, the actors in Helen's tragedy are decent — overly passionate perhaps, but not vicious. Her story, then, points out the dangers involved in passionate love; and Musidorus, at least for a while, takes the lesson to heart. It changes his attitude toward love from indifference to antipathy, so that he later explains the emotion to Pyrocles by saying:

> But this bastard Love (for indeed the name of love is most unworthily applied to so hateful a humor) as it is engendered betwixt lust and idleness; as the matter it works upon is nothing but a certain base weakness, which some gentle fools call a gentle heart; as his adjoined companions be unquietness, longings, fond comforts, faint discomforts, hopes, jealousies, ungrounded rages, causeless yieldings; so is the highest end it aspires unto, a little pleasure with much pain before, and great repentance after. (I, 78)[38]

Musidorus's attack on love shows a misogynic bias that may

itself result from his knowledge that Helen was the unwitting cause of Philoxenus's death and Amphialus's madness. This bias is clear in what he proposes Pyrocles consider in order to dissuade his friend from love: " . . . if you consider what it is, that moved you, or by what kind of creature you are moved, you shall find the cause so small, the effect so dangerous, . . . that I doubt not I shall quickly have occasion . . . to praise you for having conquered it . . . " (I, 78-79). Pyrocles immediately catches the misogynic tone here and undercuts it with the logical reply: " . . . if I be anything . . . I was come to it, born of a woman, and nursed of a woman" (I, 79). And in further defense of both women and love, Pyrocles adds that women "are capable of virtue and virtue (you yourselves say) is to be loved . . . "(I, 80). In short, Pyrocles — who has the audience with him at this point — rejects misogyny.

To a large extent, our reaction to love in the *Arcadia* will hinge on how we respond to the two sides of this debate. If we side with Musidorus, the work becomes one in which the follies of the central characters are emphasized. On the other hand, if we agree with Pyrocles, we see that the *Arcadia* shows love to be a complex, potentially disastrous but essentially virtuous emotion. Sidney, however, so structures the debate as to give Pyrocles' position the greater weight. Musidorus's attack consists of three distinct objections, each of which is effectively rebutted by Pyrocles: Musidorus objects to the transformation love has wrought in his friend; he claims that love is a bastard emotion; and he sees women as being unworthy love-objects.[39] Pyrocles' rebuttal of the last is dealt with above and is of the least consequence; he has more difficulty with the other two objections. To Musidorus's worry that " . . . this effeminate love of a woman doth so womanize a man" (I, 78) that Pyrocles' transformation from prince to Amazon is only the beginning of his degradation, Pyrocles replies that the Amazons are among the greatest of women:

> that if generally the sweetness of their dispositions did not make them see the vainness of these things, which we account glorious,

they neither want valor of mind, nor yet doth their fairness take
away their force. (I, 79)

And to Musidorus's attack on the vices of love itself, Pyrocles
argues that these are the fault not of love but of faulty lovers:

Those troublesome effects you say it breeds, be not the faults of
love, but of him that loves; as an unable vessel to bear such a liquor:
like evil eyes, not able to look on the sun; or like a weak brain,
soonest overthrown with the best wine. Even that heavenly love you
speak of, is accompanied in some hearts with hopes, griefs, longings,
and despairs. (I, 80)

While it would probably be an error to claim that Pyrocles
completely demolishes Musidorus's position, P. Albert
Duhamel is surely right when he says of Pyrocles' part in the
debate, that it "leaves the final impression that Sidney was
well aware of the probative value of Musidorus' arguments
and the fallacies to which they were subject."[40]

vi

Pyrocles' victory in the debate, however, leaves unresolved
the embarrassing question of his transvestism. To say that it
is dictated by the exigencies of the plot does not explain how
the audience is to react to it. That response will be modulated
by two factors: attitudes toward sex-disguises and attitudes
toward Amazons. Unfortunately both of these attitudes are
historically fuzzy: there are serious reasons for both accepting and repudiating both facets of Pyrocles' disguise. In her
admirable study of "The Amazons in Elizabethan Literature," Celeste Turner Wright concludes that Elizabethan
attitudes toward Amazons had been carried over from the
Middle Ages. Although the subjects of Elizabeth enjoyed the
ornamental function of Amazons in pageants and romances,
they regarded the social system of the lady warriors "as a
dangerous example of unwomanly conduct, a violation of . . .

traditional order."[41] The ambivalence that Mrs. Wright suggests in Elizabethan attitudes implies that it is futile to step outside the *Arcadia* in order to justify the claim that Pyrocles' "Amazonian disguise is a figure for the spiritual condition he has reached through allowing himself to become subject to passionate love."[42] Support for such a reading must come from within the work or not at all. Yet only Musidorus of all the Arcadian characters sees anything wrong with the Amazonian disguise and his objections are not based on a distrust of Amazons but on the womanizing effect of love.

The transvestism of Pyrocles' disguise is a different matter. It has clearly been a sore spot for Sidney's critics and they have attempted to bypass the problem in various ways. J. J. Jusserand, for example, remarks that such disguises were a cultural phenomenon: "Disguises were abundantly used in fetes and ceremonies, but they were also utilized in actual life."[43] Danby, on the other hand, argues that the transvestism is not repulsive because of its allegorical significance: "It is because of what it *means* that the transvestism is not offensive."[44] He claims that the disguise suggests Pyrocles' capability "of a synthesis of qualities that includes the womanly yet avoids the hermaphroditic."[45] This synthesis, he argues, is greater than mere masculine prowess. Of the two explanations, Danby's is preferable, depending, as it does, primarily on the text, not on the amorphous concept of contemporary public opinion. But Danby, like many critics, is too deadpan; he misses the deft touch of Sidney's humor in the passage, a touch that Rose points out: "Still it is not the emblematic significance of the costume that first strikes the reader, but its absurdity."[46] By dressing Pyrocles as Zelmane, Sidney provokes both delight and laughter; the picture is, as Rose also points out, remarkably close to the image of Hercules in woman's clothes, of which Sidney says, "for the representing of so straunge a power in Love, procures delight, and the scornefulnesse of the action, stirreth laughter" (III, 40).

The effect of laughter at this point is the creation of comic detachment from Pyrocles, suggesting the need for a critical perspective in matters of love. This in turn accords with the comparison of the Argalus-Parthenia and Amphialus-Helen episodes, 'which showed both the potential good and the potential disaster of love. The comic detachment, however, does not imply necessary repudiation of Pyrocles' stance. Clearly Musidorus's own arguments are faulty, primarily because they rest on an unthinking opposition to love and immediate repudiation would identify the audience with Musidorus's position. Morover, the detachment resulting from Pyrocles' disguise is more than counterbalanced by the overall tendency of the narrative to internalize the audience. Pyrocles is himself not entirely free of the comic detachment, as he indicates in the wry and mildly ribald remark, "Neither doubt you, because I wear a woman's apparel, I will be the more womanish, since, I assure you (for all my apparel) there is nothing I desire more, than fully to prove myself a man in this enterprise" (I, 81). This remark suggests that, if the comic detachment does in fact lead to critical thinking, Pyrocles is not the unthinking slave of passion that he is often accused of being. It moreover lends the support of self-reflection to his argument in the debate with Musidorus.

Since Pyrocles' disguise does not call forth an automatic reaction from the audience save for the rather vague "delight and laughter," the audience's response will be determined by the reasons for its adoption and the consequences of its presence. But surely if there is one response asked for by the *Arcadia* it is the acceptance and approval of Pyrocles' love of Philoclea, so that Pyrocles' success in gaining access to Basilius's lodge will be a success with which the audience has full sympathy. The only negative result of the disguise is Basilius's infatuation with his new guest,[47] but this is more of a comment on Basilius than on the disguise itself, a comment verbalized by Pyrocles:

> You never saw four score years dance up and down more lively in a young lover: now, as fine in his apparel, as if he would make me

in love with a cloak; and verse for verse with the sharpest-witted lover in Arcadia. (I, 93)

Basilius's lust parallels, as Isler points out,[48] his political failure in withdrawing from his realm and so does not indicate a flaw in Pyrocles' disguise. Finally, the young prince's marriage to Philoclea, a goal that the audience shares with him that results directly from his disguise, serves at least pragmatically to justify that disguise.

Pyrocles' disguise is an emblem of the way space is structured by psychological states and so makes explicit one of the primary concerns of Book I. The fact is most evident in the sonnet Musidorus overhears when he comes upon his disguised friend:

> Transform'd in show, but more transform'd in mind,
> I cease to strive with double conquest foil'd:
> For (woe is me) my powers all I find
> With outward force, and inward treason spoil'd.
>
> For from without came to mine eyes the blow,
> Whereto mine inward thoughts did faintly yield;
> Both these conspir'd poor Reason's overthrow;
> False in myself, thus have I lost the field.
>
> Thus are my eyes still captive to one sight;
> Thus all my thoughts are slaves to one thought still;
> Thus Reason to his servants yields his right;
> Thus is my power transform'd to your will.
>   What marvel then I take a woman's hue,
>   Since what I see, think, know is all but you?

(I, 76)

The entrance of love through the eyes — a standard Renaissance device[49] — is especially appropriate here. The lines "For from without came to mine eyes the blow, /Whereto mine inward thoughts did faintly yield" imply strongly the impact of what is out there on what is in here. This disguise itself is a variation of the book's emphasis on the structuring of space through psychological perception, an emphasis that occurs in the usual form in "Since what I see, think, know is all but you."

The same emphasis can be seen in Pyrocles' explanation to Musidorus of how he came to fall in love with Philoclea (I, 84-85). Here, however, the focus is on the effects felt by Pyrocles and on the corresponding changes in his attitudes that lead to his decision to disguise himself as an Amazon. First, he saw the painting of Philoclea who, it turns out, both resembles and surpasses "the Lady Zelmane, whom so well I loved . . . " (I, 84). Further explanations concerning "the Lady Zelmane" are not given us until Book II and are here unnecessary because this simple reference is enought to explain Pyrocles' immediate response to the portrait. The explanation of Philoclea's present confined circumstances provided by Kalander added to Pyrocles' response until he found his attitudes changing from pity to tenderness to love. Finally, he says, " . . . I came to the degree of uncertain wishes, and that those wishes grew to unquiet longings, when I could fix my thoughts upon nothing, but that within little varying, they should end with Philoclea . . . " (I, 85). Pyrocles' speech balances his song to the extent that it shows the operation of the world on him. The lavish attention to details, moreover, tends to fix not only our attention but our sympathy on Pyrocles' plight. Thus we are the more likely to give him the nod in his debate with Musidorus.

Curiously enough, one consequence of Pyrocles' disguise serves to demonstrate that the ability to see through appearances does not necessarily lead to right or moral action. Gynecia discovers right away that the supposed Amazon is in fact a man, a suitor for her daughter. But instead of exposing Pyrocles as an intruder in the royal retreat, Gynecia falls in love with him. This is not entirely unfortunate to Pyrocles' plans for, as he points out, " . . . must I confess, that one way her love doth me pleasure: for since it was my foolish fortune, or unfortunate folly, to be known by her, that keeps me from bewraying me to Basilius" (I, 94). On the other hand, Gynecia's love, coupled with Basilius's love for the disguised Pyrocles and Pyrocles' for Philoclea, results in a scene of high comedy of which Pyrocles is not entirely unappreciative:

> Truly it were a notable dumb show of Cupid's kingdom, to see my eyes (languishing with overvehement longing) direct themselves to Philoclea: and Basilius as busy about me as a bee, and indeed as cumbersome; making such vehement suits to me, who neither could if I would; nor would if I could, help him: while the terrible wit of Gynecia, carried with the beer of violent love, runs through us all. And so jealous is she of my love to her daughter, that I could never yet begin to open my mouth to the unevitable Philoclea, but that her unwished presence gave my tale a conclusion, before it had a beginning. (I, 94)[50]

The comedy notwithstanding, the actions of Basilius and Gynecia are a serious threat not only to Pyrocles' plans but to the family structure that the *Arcadia* appears to assume as a good. Both Basilius and Gynecia are attempting to establish an adulterous liaison, the one blindly accepting Pyrocles at face value and the other seeing through his disguise to his essential masculinity. Evidently, then, it is not misinterpretation of the external that leads one astray, but some sort of propensity to wrongdoing inherent in the individual.[51] Sidney is careful to establish such propensities early in his presentation of each of his characters. Gynecia's vulnerability is established in Kalander's description of her to Musidorus: she is "of most unspotted chastity, but of so working a mind, and so vehement spirits, as a man may say, it was happy she took a good course: for otherwise it would have been terrible" (I, 20).

vii

The lust of Gynecia and Basilius for the disguised Pyrocles serves as a preparation for the tournament of Phalantus, and the tournament is a comment on their lust. Unlike the profound love between Argalus and Parthenia and the overly passionate love borne by Helen for Amphialus, the relationship between Phalantus and Artesia is clearly established as superficial and merely fashionable. Youthful courtiers, argues Basilius, "make themselves believe they love at the first liking of a likely beauty; loving, because they will love for want of other business, not because they feel indeed that divine power . . . " (I, 98). Basilius's explanation of the superficial relationship between Phalantus and Artesia goes a long way toward explaining his own behavior. If young people "will love for want of other business, not because they feel indeed that divine power," it is not surprising that one effect of Basilius's withdrawal from responsibility should be that he would consider a diversion with an Amazon. By implication, then, Basilius's remarks provide another connection between the erotic and political motifs by showing that political abdication can lead to an erotic entanglement.

The Phalantus-Artesia relationship shows as well that actions which in another context are ethical can compound an adolescent mistake. Phalantus, in the spirit of the passion which he is imitating, makes excessive vows, which Artesia forces him to keep. Artesia charges Phalantus "to go with her through all the courts of Greece, and with the challenge now made, to give her beauty the principality over all other" (I, 99). Although Phalantus has come to recognize that he does not truly love Artesia and although he knows that his sister, Helen, and Pamela, Philoclea, and Parthenia all have better claim to the title of "Peerless Beauty" than Artesia, he agrees to the quest because " . . . his promise had bound him prentice . . . and therefore [he] went on, as his faith, rather than love, did lead him" (I, 100). The dilemma is clear and is the product of his own lack of initial sincerity and foresight. Moreover, it suggests that absolute and abstract codes build into themselves inflexibilities, the consequences of which are as disastrous as those which follow a refusal to live by any acceptable code. And this problem of erotic motivation is reflected in Basilius's retreat.

Phalantus's tournament again indicates the interrelationship between the ordering of space and the psychology of
perception, this time showing how perception is affected
from the outside. Each of the portraits in "the painted mus-
ter of an eleven conquered beauties" is a representation not
merely of physical appearance but of psychological and
social status as well. For example, the portrait of Parthenia
shows both her great beauty and her profound modesty:

> Of a far differing (though esteemed equal) beauty, was the fair
> Parthenia, who next waited on Artesia's triumph, though far better
> she might have sat in the throne. For in her everything was goodly,
> and stately; yet so, that it might seem that great-mindedness was but
> the ancient-bearer to the humbleness. For her great grey eye, which
> might seem full of her own beauty, a large, and exceedingly fair
> forehead, with all the rest of her face and body, cast in the mold of
> nobleness; was yet so attired, as might show, the mistress thought it
> either not to deserve, or not to need any exquisite decking, having
> no adorning but cleanliness; and so far from all art, that it was full
> of carelessness: unless that carelessness itself (in spite of itself) grew
> artificial. (I, 103-4)

The qualities embodied in Parthenia's portrait are those noted
in her personality during the Argalus-Parthenia episode and
are confirmed by her refusal to let Argalus redeem her portrait because " . . . she desired to be beautiful in nobody's
eye but his; and that she would rather mar her face as evil as
ever it was, than that it should be a cause to make Argalus
put on armor" (I, 104).

In marked contrast to the portrait of Parthenia is that of
Artaxia. In this portrait, Artaxia's malevolent personality
shows through her surface beauty:

> After her [the princess of Elis] was the goodly Artaxia, great
> Queen of Armenia, a lady upon whom nature bestowed, and well
> placed her most delightful colors; and withal, had proportioned her
> without any fault, quickly to be discovered by the senses, yet alto-
> gether seemed not to make up that harmony, that Cupid delights in,
> the reason whereof might seem a mannish countenance, which over-
> threw that lovely sweetness, the noblest power of womankind, far
> fitter to prevail by parley, than by battle. (I, 102)

Clearly one of the functions of this description is to modulate the audience's response to Artaxia in preparation for her introduction in Book II. The technique used here is not particularly subtle — praise followed by significant qualification — but neither is Artaxia particularly subtle. At any rate, Sidney is careful to control his descriptions so as to indicate each lady's personality and to prepare the audience for her appearance later. This latter is important to the narrative structure, for, as Davis notes, the procession not only reviews the women introduced in Book I, but also introduces the women who figure so prominently in the retrospective narratives of Book II.[52]

Phalantus's tournament prevents us from overstressing the chivalric component of the *Arcadia*. The initial jousts are rather colorless affairs, as can be seen from the first tilt:

> But the other knight, by name Nestor, by birth an Arcadian, and in affection vowed to the fair shepherdess, was all in black, with fire burning both upon his armor and horse. His impresa in his shield, was a fire made of juniper, with this word, "More easy, and more sweet." But this hot knight was cooled with a fall, which at the third course he received of Phalantus, leaving his picture to keep company with the other of the same stamp. he going away remedylessly chafing at his rebuke. (I, 105-6).

In the midst of the young knights' futile attempts to defend the portraits of the ladies, a young shepherd comes forward in defense of Urania. Described as "a shepherd stripling (for his height made him more than a boy, and his face would not allow him a man) brown of complexion (whether by nature or by the sun's familiarity) but very lovely withal" (I, 106), he pleads with Basilius to

> Let me be dressed as they be, and my heart gives me, I shall tumble him on the earth: for indeed he might as well say, that a cowslip is as white as a lily: or else I care not let him come with his great staff, and I with this in my hand, and you shall see what I can do to him. (I, 107)

Basilius's response to the plea — "laughing at his earnestness, he bade him be content" (I, 107) — shows the audience how the tourney as a whole should be taken. For what has happened is that the potentially serious and significant part of human life summed up in the word *love* verges on the ludicrous in the adolescence of this contest. Without denying the validity or significance of the erotic motive, then, Sidney again manages to suggest the need for critical detachment and in so doing provides a comment on Basilius's own earnest courtship of the disguised Pyrocles — a comment ironically made by Basilius himself.

The sequence of events that closes the tournament carries on this underlying sense of the ridiculous. An "ill-apparelled knight" enters and strikes Phalantus's shield as the signal of challenge, "but as he let his sword fall upon it, another knight, all in black came rustling in, who struck the shield almost as soon as he, and so strongly, that he broke the shield in two . . . " (I, 109). The two knights immediately begin contesting for the right to fight first. Phalantus, angry because his shield has been defaced, joins in, and what ought by the rules of chivalry to have been formal joust becomes a comic melee described in terms of dance:

> who ever saw a matachin dance to imitate fighting, this was a fight that did imitate the matachin: for they being but three that fought, everyone had two adversaries, striking him, who struck the third, and revenging perhaps that of him, which he had received of the other. (I, 109)

Basilius parts the combatants, but before the issue can be settled a fourth knight, "the halting knight," arrives, complaining "to Basilius, demanding justice on the black knight, for having by force taken away the picture of Pamela from him . . . " (I, 110). Although the episode is resolved when the "halting knight" is sent to "learn of *Æsculapius* that he was not fit for Venus" (I, 110) and the "ill-apparelled knight," granted precedence for first striking the shield, defeats Phalantus,[53] it surely must be viewed in a comic light. This in turn suggests that, like love, chivalry demands critical detachment and that the *Arcadia* is not simply a chivalric romance on the order of, say, *Floris and Blancheflour* or *Ywain and Gawayn*.

After his success at Phalantus's tournament, Pyrocles — who is the "ill-apparelled knight" — encounters Musidorus disguised as the shepherd Dorus singing "these few verses":

> Come shepherd's weeds, become your master's mind:
> Yield outward show, what inward change he tries:
> Nor be abash'd, since this guest you find,
> Whose strongest hope in your weak comfort lies.
> Come shepherd's weeds, attend my woeful cries:
> Disuse yourselves from sweet Menalcas' voice:
> For other be those tunes which sorrow ties,
> From those clear notes which freely may rejoice.
>   Then pour out plaint, and in one word say this:
>   Helpless his plaint, who soils himself of bliss.
>
>   (I, 113)

Discovering that it is love that has wrought this transformation in his friend, Pyrocles cannot resist the urge to tease Musidorus for reversing his earlier position on love: "Remember that love is a passion; and that a worthy man's reason must ever have the masterhood" (I, 113-14). This sequence obviously parallels the sequence in which Musidorus discovers the disguised Pyrocles, so much so that Pyrocles wonders

> whether the goddess of those woods had such a power to transform everybody, or whether, as in all enterprises else he had done, he [Musidorus] meant thus to match her [Pyrocles-Zelmane] in this new alteration. (I, 113)

Of course the former supposition is correct; but working these transformations is the power of love, which has become disordered with the departure of Urania. The transformations are at once internal — the "inward change" — and manifested in a change in outward appearance — the "shepherd's weeds." The parallelism between the two discovery sequences emphasizes the error of Musidorus's earlier position when taken as an absolute and again suggests that reality is the product of inside and outside.

viii

By the last chapter of the first book, then, all of the main characters have been gathered together in Basilius's retreat. Moreover, the primary erotic lines have been drawn: Pyrocles, disguised as the Amazon Zelmane, is in love with Philoclea but is himself being pursued by both Gynecia and Basilius while Musidorus, disguised as the shepherd Dorus, is in love with Pamela. Besides bringing the last of the characters, Musidorus, into the fold, the final chapter looks forward to the conflicts that will follow, particularly the struggle between the forces of Basilius and those of Cecropia for control of Arcadia. This anticipation appears in Gynecia's reflection on the apology sent by Cecropia for the accidental release of the bear and lion that had threatened the lives of Pamela and Philoclea; since Cecropia's son is the next male heir to Basilius's throne, Gynecia "saw no reason, but that she might conjecture, it proceeded rather of some mischievous practice, than of misfortune" (I, 125). Finally the last chapter leads directly into the eclogues, which in a way sum up the motifs and narrative methodology of the first book.

The opening lines of the shepherds underline the erotic motif of Book I, especially insofar as that motif is manifested in the stories of Argalus and Parthenia and of Amphialus and Helen:

> Then would they cast away their pipes; and holding hand in hand, dance as it were in a brawl, by the only cadence of their voices, which they would use in singing some short couplets, whereto the one half beginning, the other half should answer, as the one half saying:
> "We love, and have our loves rewarded."
> The others would answer:
> "We love, and are no whit regarded."
> The first again:

"We find most sweet affection's snare."
With like tune it should be as in a choir sent back again:
        "That sweet, but sour despairful care."
A third time likewise thus:
        "Who can despair, whom hope doth bear?"
The answer:
        "And who can hope that feels despair?"
Then all joining their voices, and dancing a faster measure, they
would conclude with some such words:
        "As without breath, no pipe doth moan:
        No music kindly without love."

                                                          (I, 126-27)

The dancing itself is emblematic of the interrelationship of
the lovers of the main narrative line, who move apart, together, apart, and finally come together in the center of the
dance, Basilius's retreat. Moreover, the first line sung by the
shepherds can be said to sum up the story of Argalus and
Parthenia, while the second line sums up the story of Amphialus and Helen. Finally, the last two lines of the song stress, just
as Book I has stressed, the erotic motif as the fundamental
cause for the actions of the characters of Arcadia.

    The erotic motif is also stressed in the ensuing poetic inter-
change between Lalus and Musidorus. Lalus's praise of Kala,
however, differs from Musidorus's of his unnamed beloved,
especially in its comparative freedom from psychological
effect. It tends to stress the outer landscape rather than the
inner state of the lover. In this singing match Musidorus wins
a double victory. Simply in terms of poetic construction he
matches and surpasses his rival.[54] And in terms of the ground
rules of the contest, Musidorus wins the laurel by best demonstrating that he "deserveth most compassion" through his
stressing the psychological effects of love on the lover.

    The singing match is followed immediately by the young
shepherd's[55] curious beast fable, which is important primarily
because it introduces into the eclogues the second major
theme of the Arcadia, the political theme. Two features of
this poem are significant to an interpretation of the Arcadia:
first, a balance is assumed to be necessary between will and

reason; second, the animals' request to Jove upsets their society much as Basilius's reliance on the oracle upsets the Arcadian society. Languet's remarks on music make clear that Sidney, unlike some of his critics, was careful to grant the place of both reason and will instead of slighting one for the other: "He said the music best th'ilke powers pleas'd/Was jump concord between our wit and will" (I, 133). Moreover, in the beast fable, which makes up the body of the poem, the beasts begin in an ordered and ideal society:

> The beasts had sure some beastly policy:
> For nothing can endure where order n'is.
> For once the lion by the lamb did lie;
> The fearful hind the leopard did kiss:
> Hurtless was tiger's paw and serpent's hiss.
> > This think I well, the beasts with courage clad
> > Like senators a harmless empire had.
>
> (I, 134)

But not quite content with their lot, the beasts pleaded with Jove for a king, a request to which Jove accedes in spite of his wisdom.

> Jove wisely said (for wisdom wisely says):
> "O beasts, take heed what you of me desire.
> Rulers will think all things made them to please,
> And soon forget the swink due to their hire;
> But since you will, part of my heav'nly fire
> > I will you lend; the rest yourselves must give,
> > That it both seen and felt may with you live."
>
> (I, 134)

The result is the creation of man and is, predictably, disaster for the beasts. Surely the parallels between this fable and Basilius's actions are obvious: like the beasts, Basilius has turned to a divine source to help him rule both himself and his society; like the beasts, he has ignored advice against this particular action (the advice given him by Philanax); and, as in the beast fable, a consequence of Basilius's choice is the potential disruption of Arcadian society. In this way Sidney manages to tie the eclogues into the political theme of the prose narrative.[5][6]

Finally, the song composed by Strephon and Claius discussed earlier, "Ye Goatherd Gods," shows in the eclogues the way the sense of space is structured according to the psychological state of the perceiver. In short, the eclogues of the first book reintroduce themes and motifs that have played a dominant role in the rest of that book.

Notes

1. Myrick, p. 136.

2. Alan D. Isler, however, does take an exception of sorts when he argues: "But it could be argued that the old *Arcadia*, too, begins *in medias res*, for had it begun *ab ovo*, it would have had to begin with the birth of the heroes rather than with the situation in Arcadia" ("Heroic Poetry and Sidney's Two *Arcadias*," *PMLA* 83 [1968] : 371). This seems to be merely a quibble and one with which Sidney would not have agreed: "Where nowe would one of our Tragedie writers begin, but with the deliverie of the childe?" (III, 39).

3. Rodney Delasanta, *The Epic Voice* (the Hague, 1967), p. 30. Much of the material in this paragraph depends heavily upon Delasanta's discussion of delegated narration (pp. 26-36).

4. *Ibid*., p. 33.

5. It is tempting to use the word *natural* here, but this temptation must be avoided, because *natural* and its opposite *unnatural* or *artistic* (depending on whether one prefers the revised or original version) tend to be evaluative words. Although preferences concerning the two *Arcadias* are certainly possible, and may even be admirable, the issue at hand is function rather than merit; hence my method must be analytic rather than normative.

6. Rose, pp. 37-38.

7. Neil L. Rudenstein, *Sidney's Poetic Development* (Cambridge, Mass., 1967), p. 30.

8. Thus Jon S. Lawry can claim that the *Arcadia* proceeds by means of "a processional accumulation of pictures from the past which will guide characters in the present as they shape the future" (p. 157). On the function of the retrospective narratives, which will be dealt with more fully in chapter 3, see Nancy Rothwax Lindheim's discussion of the Renaissance distinction between fable and episode in her "Vision, Revision, and the 1593 Text of the *Arcadia*," *ELR* 2 (1972): 136-47.

9. Davis, *passim*.

10. Even a cursory perusal of A. G. D. Wiles's parallel plot summaries will substantiate this ("Parallel Analysis of the Two Versions of Sidney's *Arcadia*," *SP* 39 [1942]: 175-80).

11. The major additions include the complaint of Strephon and Claius, the love of Argalus and Parthenia, the Helots' rebellion in Laconia, Helen of Corinth's unhappy love for Amphialus, and Phalantus's tourney; the two deletions are the oracle's reply to Basilius and the early history of Pyrocles and Musidorus. The two omissions are brought into the *Arcadia* when the appropriate circumstances arise for their insertion in the story: Basilius reveals the prophecy of the oracle when he is rebuking Philanax (I, 326-28) and Musidorus reveals his and Pyrocles' origins during his mock wooing of Mopsa (I, 151-66).

12. It is significant that it is in the second book that this and other allusions to past events are cleared up, for the second book, unlike the first, is concerned with the meaning of events in time.

13. As the text of the *Arcadia* stands, these are left unresolved. But it seems entirely likely that, had Sidney lived to complete his revision, both love relationships would have been satisfactorily resolved. Both are in a way emblematic of the greater themes of the *Arcadia*. Successful resolution of the political crisis, which involves Amphialus's mother, Cecropia, could be mirrored in the marriage between him and Helen, Queen of Corinth, and the amatory adventures of the two princes conclude with the symbolic return of Urania. See Katherine Duncan-Jones, "Sidney's Urania," *RES* n.s. 17 (1966): 132, for the slightly less concrete suggestion that Sidney might have brought Urania back in at the end of the *New Arcadia* and cleared up her mystery.

14. Katherine Duncan-Jones, however, conjectures one other appearance of Strephon and Claius. She thinks that the unidentified knights who come to the rescue of Musidorus late in Book III are in fact the two shepherds (130-31). The conjecture, attractive as it is, does not, however, lift Strephon and Claius out of the league of minor characters as the work stands and it does not explain what their future involvement, if any, would have been.

15. Myrick, p. 115.

16. *Ibid.*, p. 116.

17. Duncan-Jones, p. 130.

18. Friedrich Brie, *Sidney's "Arcadia": Eine Studie zur Englischen Renaissance* (Strasburg, 1918), pp. 280-81.

19. Wiles, p. 168.

20. For a rare reading of the work as historical allegory, see Edwin Greenlaw's two articles: "Sidney's *Arcadia* as an example of Elizabethan Allegory," *Kittredge*

Anniversary Papers (Boston, 1913), pp. 327-37, and "The Captivity Episode in Sidney's 'Arcadia,' " *The Manly Anniversary Studies* (Chicago, 1923), pp. 54-63. Greenlaw's reading has not yet, however, been widely accepted.

21. Davis, p. 88. Davis's neoplatonic vision has recently been supported by Myron Turner, "The Disfigured Face of Nature: Image and Metaphor in the Revised *Arcadia*," *ELR* 2 (1972): 116-35.

22. Davis, p. 86. For the theory of the neoplatonic ladder of love applied to Pyrocles and Musidorus, see Davis's chapter entitled "Amorous Courting," particularly pp. 73-82.

23. A. C. Hamilton comes to a similar conclusion in his review article "Recent Studies in the English Renaissance," *SEL* 9 (1969): 77. Hamilton notices the same sort of phenomenon in the *Astrophil and Stella* ("Sidney's *Astrophel and Stella* as a Sonnet Sequence," *ELH* 36 [1969]: 59-87. In the *ELR* aritcle "Sidney's *Arcadia* as Prose Fiction: Its Relation to Its Sources," he discusses precisely this scene and, although he suggests that Claius is the "elder 'pastor' or guide," he also notes that " . . . Strephon's lament and Claius' consolation are balanced and discriminated . . . " (p. 50).

24. Rose, pp. 43-44. See also Robert Kimbrough, p. 127.

25. Rose, p. 45.

26. Duncan-Jones, p. 132.

27. A corollary to this interpretation is that the kind of scholarly studies of Urania's name by Lily Bess Campbell (*Divine Poetry and Drama in Sixteenth-Century England* [Berkeley, 1959], pp. 74-83) and John M. Steadman (" 'Meaning' and 'Name': Some Renaissance Interpretations of Urania," *NM* 64 [1963]: 209-32) are more generally likely to obscure matters than to clarify them. Miss Duncan-Jones's article is an exception, primarily because her interest is explicitly in Sidney and because for her the *Arcadia* is the primary text and her other sources only secondary.

28. *Sidney's Poetry: Contexts and Interpretations* (Cambridge, Mass., 1965), p. 79.

29. *The English Epic and Its Background* (London, 1954; New York, 1966), p. 303. See also Myron Turner's discussion of the shipwreck as an image of "the disfigured face of nature" (119-21).

30. *Lectures on the Literature of the Age of Elizabeth and Characters of Shakespear's Plays* (London, 1901), pp. 205-6.

31. "Primitivistic Motifs in Sidney's *Arcadia*," *Papers of the Michigan Academy of Science, Arts, and Letters* 45 (1960): 367.

32. Primitivism is used here in the sense defined by Arthur O. Lovejoy and

George Boas as "the discontent of the civilized with civilization, or with some conspicuous and characteristic feature of it. It is the belief of men living in a relatively highly evolved and complex cultural condition that a life far simpler and less sophisticated in some or all respects is a more desirable life" (*Primitivism and Related Ideas in Antiquity* [Baltimore, Md., 1935], p. 7).

33. Gohn, pp. 370-71.

34. It is tempting to call this first theme the ethical theme rather than the erotic, but to do so runs the risk of over-schematicizing on the one hand and over-intellectualizing on the other. And "erotic" is used here with full recognition of the seriousness of amatory behavior in the *Arcadia*.

35. John F. Danby also draws a distinction between the erotic and political movements in Sidney's work. "There are, then, two separate but related spheres in the Sidneian universe. One is the outer world of public events, the other the inner world of private affections. One is heroical, the other amatorious. One is the sphere of magnanimity, the other the sphere for the exercise of patience" (*Elizabethan and Jacobean Poets: Studies in Sidney, Shakespeare, Beaumont and Fletcher* [London, 1952; 1965], p. 51). In his perceptive study, Danby argues that the *Arcadia* synthesizes in much the manner of dialectics these two opposing spheres. But the erotic and political are not so much thesis and antithesis as parallel fields of behavior. In any given instance they may be either in opposition to one another or in a complementary relationship; but they are, in the *Arcadia*, intertwined and never quite separable.

36. "Machiavelli and Sidney: *The Arcadia of 1590*," *SP* 47 (1950): 162.

37. The consequences of such an involvement are made clear by Pyrocles in his suggestion, cited above, that the Helots return Clitophon and Kalander.

38. Lorna Challis notes that the effectiveness of this period is at least in part the consequence of its structure: "The basis of the structure of the sentence is the logic of the argument, but the sentence is also designed for rhetorical effectiveness in that the accumulation of members having the same grammatical and logical function is a way of conveying urgency" ("The Use of Oratory in Sidney's *Arcadia*," *SP* 62 [1964]: 565). She fails, however, to note the underlying misognic bias of Musidorus's argument, since that is beside her point.

39. P. Albert Duhamel gives an elaborate rhetorical analysis of Musidorus's argument ("Sidney's *Arcadia* and Elizabethan Rhetoric," *SP* 45 [1948]: 144-48).

40. *Ibid.*, p. 148.

41. *SP* 37 (1940): 456. Spenser, in *The Faerie Queene*, was able to accommodate both views of the Amazons by including Britomart and Radigund as foils to one another. Sidney's work, on the other hand, does not show this balance, and Celeste Turner Wright includes it among those which have a positive view of Amazons.

42. Mark Rose, "Sidney's Womanish Man," *RES* 15 (1964): 363.

43. *The English Novel in the Time of Shakespeare* (London, 1890; New York, 1966), p. 328. Jusserand adds in his footnote to this passage the literary traditions behind this disguise: "The taste for these fancies had been handed down from the Middle Ages; ladies following as pages their own lovers, unknown to them, abound in the French mediaeval literature . . . " (p. 238 n1).

44. Danby, p. 57.

45. *Ibid*., p. 56.

46. *Heroic Love*, p. 51. This represents a softening of his earlier position expressed in "Sidney's Womanish Man." It might also be noticed, at least in passing, that the humor of the disguise does not bear up well under critical discussion or under such labels as *transvestism*, probably because of the delicate touch with which Sidney handles the humor in order not to censure Pyrocles. In this, Sidney's work differs from Ben Jonson's more heavy-handed *Epicoene*.

47. Two other apparent drawbacks to the disguise are more apparent than real. Gynecia's lust for the disguised Pyrocles is in a crucial way independent of the disguise itself, for she sees through it. The dilemma felt by Philoclea later in Book II, when she thinks that she has fallen in love with a woman, is too complex to handle fully here and will be treated in detail in chapter 3; it may tentatively be claimed that the dilemma is only apparent, however, since "Zelmane" is actually a man, whose main purpose is the courtship of Philoclea.

48. "Moral Philosophy and the Family in Sidney's *Arcadia*," *HLQ* 31 (1968): 365.

49. For example, see Rosalind's ladder of love in *As You Like It:* "O, I know where you are: nay, 'tis true: there was never any thing so sudden but the fight of two rams and Caesar's thrasonical brag of 'I came, saw, and overcame:' for your brother and my sister no sooner met but they looked, no sooner looked but they loved, no sooner loved but they sighed, no sooner sighed but they asked one another the reason, no sooner knew the reason but they sought the remedy; and in these degrees have they made a pair of stairs to marriage which they will climb incontinent, or else be incontinent before marriage: they are in the very wrath of love and they will together; clubs cannot part them" (V. ii, 32-45). Citations from Shakespeare in my text are to *The Complete Works of Shakespeare*, ed. Hardin Craig (Chicago, 1961).

50. This scene is an example of Sidney's use of comedy without the corresponding detachment. Detachment is inhibited here because the audience's ironic perspective is shared by Pyrocles.

51. One must, of course, distinguish degrees of wrongdoing in the *Arcadia*, for there is clearly a difference between the characters who are merely fallible,

Basilius and Gynecia, for example, and those who are fundamentally evil, such as Demagoras and Cecropia.

52.   "Thematic Unity in the *New Arcadia*," *SP* 57 (1960): 125.

53.   Phalantus expresses relief at being freed from his ill-advised obligation to Artesia by his defeat, much to the amusement of Basilius: " '. . . I think the loss of such a mistress [as Artesia] will prove a great gain,' and so concluded, to the sport of Basilius, to see young folks love, that came in masked with so great pomp, go out with so little constancy" (I, 111). Basilius's reaction, of course, is another ironic reflection of how the audience ought to react to his behavior.

54.   In his commentary to his peom, Ringler admirably explains the contest in terms of poetic form (*Poems*, pp. 385-86).

55.   In the *Old Arcadia* the young shepherd is called Philisides and is perhaps a transparency for Sidney himself.

56.   The best single discussion of the eclogues is probably Elizabeth Dipple's "The 'Fore Conceit' of Sidney's Eclogues," *Literary Monographs* 1 (Madison, 1967): 3-47. She rightly points out that the eclogues as they appear in the editions of 1590 and 1593 do not represent Sidney's intent and chooses to treat the eclogues as they appear in the *Old Arcadia*. A study such as this must, however, forgo the luxury of using the eclogues of the *Old Arcadia* and use those of either 1590 or 1593. I have chosen the arrangement of 1590 because that of the eclogues in 1593 seems to have been dictated, at least in part, by Mary Sidney's desire to save her brother's poetry for posterity and therefore fits the *New Arcadia* less well.

3

Book II and the Structure of Time

i

Of the two-and-a-half books of the *Arcadia* that Sidney
had completed before his death, the second is by far the
most complicated. The events covered in the main narration
occur within a few days, while the events in the delegated
narrations, which fill well over half the book, cover events
from before the princes' births to after their arrival in Arcadia. Perhaps this is the book S. L. Wolff has in mind when he
speaks of Sidney's "re-weaving the Old Arcadia upon the
loom of Heliodorus."[1] The metaphor of the loom and
tapestry, though perhaps doing justice to Sidney's difficult
task of rewriting the *Old Arcadia*, suggests the significance
of spatial relations, whereas Book II has at its core the issue

of temporal relations. The complex structure of delegated narrations stresses the influence of past events and so builds out of time a pyramidlike structure according to which any present event is the product of a matrix of preceding events. Thus, while the central narration is linear, the complex temporal interrelationships posited in the delegated narrations are geometric.[2] Moreover, the structure of the book as a whole reflects this distinction between simple temporal progression and complex temporal causality. Musidorus's narrations at the beginning of Book II are simpler in both form and substance than Pyrocles' narrations at its close.

In many ways the problem of perspectives in time is far more complicated than that of perspectives in space.[3] Clearly a point in space is easier to localize than a point in time. In a narrative such as the *Arcadia*, moreover, one can neither utilize physicists' device of spatializing time nor reduce time to quantitative units. Sidney had to deal with time by some method that was amenable to his narrative; he chose to present complex causal chains. This has a double effect: it clearly suggests that the significance of an event is determined at least in part by when it occurs in causal chains and it also suggests that present being entails a convergence of past events and future possibilities. Quinones' remark about the "present" in Montaigne may apply almost as well to Sidney's *Arcadia*: "By analogy with eternity, the present is not merely the moment at hand; it is summary and all-embracing, compressing in the depth of its vision a completed and rounded-out picture of human existence."[4]

The change in focus from spatial relationships in Book I to temporal and causal relationships in Book II is marked not only by a change in the presentation of events, but also by a stylistic change. The static, pictorial qualities of the first book are used sparingly in the second; verbs of action are substituted for verbs of sight. Events tend less to be presented and tend more to happen, and this is true even of the retrospective narratives. The stormy shipwreck described by Musidorus in his narrative to Pamela, for example, is in

marked contrast to the shipwreck scene in Book I. Instead
of in a scene of destruction, we participate in the very act of
destruction:

> with an unbelieved violence . . . the ship ran upon it [a rock]; and
> seeming willinger to perish than to have her course stayed, redoubled
> her blows, till she had broken herself in pieces; and as it were tearing
> out her own bowels to feed the sea's greediness, left nothing within
> it but despair of safety, and expectation of a loathsome end. (I, 193)

The activity of the ship crashing itself upon the rock and dis-
emboweling itself carries with it the sense of time as an essential attribute of process, which corresponds to the overall
narrative style of Book II.

ii

The opening chapters of Book II recall the situation established in the first book: Pyrocles, disguised as the Amazon
Zelmane, loves Philoclea but is being pursued by her parents
while Musidorus, disguised as the shepherd Dorus, loves
Pamela but finds that the churlish Dametas and his family
interfere with his courtship. Gynecia's love complaints open
the book and are followed immediately by Pyrocles' love complaints. Gynecia thereupon declares her passion for the disguised prince but the two are fortuitously interrupted by
Basilius singing his love complaint. The sequence, then, is a
sort of comic dance and a burlesque of love entanglements.
As such, it warns the audience that, however serious love itself may be, its effects are frequently absurd. The comedy of
this erotic quadrangle does not escape Pyrocles: "Truly Love,
I must needs say thus much on thy behalf; thou hast employed my love there, where all love is deserved; and for
recompence hast sent me more love than ever I desired"
(I, 151). Pyrocles' self-awareness at this point protects him
from the criticism implicit in the scene's comedy.

Pyrocles' problems with Gynecia and Basilius are followed

by Musidorus's tale of his partial success with Pamela. Having discovered the limitations of his disguise, "that a shepherd's service was but considered of as from a shepherd, and the acceptation limited to no further proportion, than of a good servant" (I, 153), he hits on the ruse of courting Pamela in the person of Mopsa,[5] a ruse that Pamela sees through quickly enough. Although the mock courtship attracts Pamela's attention to the "sport of wit" (I, 155), it is not enough to attract her to Musidorus. And while Pamela finds his personal qualifications attractive, she requires knowledge of his estate because " . . . it is not for us [women] to play the philosophers, in seeking out your hidden virtues: since that, which in a wise prince would be counted wisdom, in us will be taken for a light-grounded affection . . . " (I, 158). Implicit in Pamela's qualification is the idea that a man's present identity is a function of his past, including both his family tree and his personal exploits. This is the first significant indication of the manner in which past events can influence present situations. Moreover, it provides a *raison d'être* for Musidorus's narratives that are to follow.

Responding to Pamela's request for more information, Musidorus presents a summary autobiography in the as-if form of "a story, which happened in this same country long since . . . whereby you shall see that my estate is not so contemptible, but that a prince hath been content to take the like upon him . . . " (I, 159). To increase the rhetorical effect of this summary biography, he proceeds obliquely to offer proof, "a red spot, bearing figure (as they tell me) of a lion's paw" (I, 163), that he is the Musidorus whose tale he has just told.[6] Pamela, of course, understands immediately who "is my Dorus fallen out to be" (I, 177) and, as she tells her sister, cannot "without the detestable stain of ungratefulness abstain from loving him, who . . . is content so to abase himself, as to become Dametas' servant for my sake" (I, 178). Because Musidorus will not learn of the quality of Pamela's response until Book III[7] and because the revelation of Pamela's love occurs in one of the rare moments of the main narrative of Books I and II when the focus is not on either one of the two princes, the revelation is of particular significance. It creates discrepant awareness in order to alleviate the tension that the audience might feel if unaware of how successful Musidorus's suit has been.[8] Moreover, Pamela's balanced reasons for loving him stress the importance of Musidorus's past. The revelation itself is therefore an early indication of the way the present builds on the past.

Time elapses, however, between Musidorus's summary narrative and the revelation that Pamela returns his love. During this interval occurs the accident in which Gynecia is injured and Philoclea's psychological turmoil over what appear to be lesbian desires. Though the former will ultimately allow Pyrocles and his love to get together, the latter has more immediate importance. The long passage that deals with Philoclea's falling in love begins with a rare editorial comment by the narrator:

> And alas (sweet Philoclea) how hath my pen till now forgot thy passions, since to thy memory principally all this long matter is intended? Pardon the slackness to come to those woes, which having caused in others, thou didst feel in thyself. (I, 168-69)

The effect of the narrator's intrusion at this point differs curiously from the narrative bridges in the *Old Arcadia*;[9] instead of externalizing the audience, this intrusion reinforces the internalization of the audience in several ways. In the first place, it is inner-directed rather than outer-directed; the remarks are directed at Philoclea rather than at the audience and this implies that the narrator, and hence the audience, is inside the sequence with the characters rather than above it. And although a girl in love with a man she thinks is a woman is clearly a fit subject for detached comedy, the narrative intrusion allies the audience's sympathy with Philoclea and mutes the satiric force of its laughter, which comes not at her expense but with sympathy with her problem and with awareness that it is no problem at all, as she will shortly learn.

The description of how Philoclea fell in love with Pyrocles

(I, 169-71), which follows hard on the narrator's interruption, obviously parallels Pyrocles' own description of how he fell in love with her (I, 84-85). Though the later description may be called a kind of set piece, Philoclea's description is remarkably long even for the *Arcadia*. By comparison with it, the similar passages in Book I suggest that falling in love is virtually instantaneous. The difference may be explained in part by the difference between the emphasis of Book I and that of Book II; the emphasis in Book II on temporality and causality is reflected here by the strong sense that falling in love is process, that it occurs in time. This fact is slighted in the earlier descriptions of falling in love. The very length of Philoclea's description and its wealth of detail, moreover, shares a function with the narrative intrusion; they ally the audience's sympathy with Philoclea and give a felt reality to the force of love. The possibility of an unfavorable response to Philoclea's love is thereby reduced.

The fact that Philoclea's love object is, to all appearances, a woman vexes the princess and amuses the audience. Although Philoclea is not cognizant of "Zelmane's" masculinity, her mother's example "greatly fortified her desires, to see, that her mother had the like desires" (I, 171). This example offers Philoclea both hope and justification for her own emotions, for her mother either "sees a possibility in that which I think impossible, or else impossible loves need not misbecome me" (I, 174-75). Although Philoclea's argument is, on its face, a rationalization for an illicit love, it is psychologically realistic and is rhetorically acceptable since there is indeed "a possibility in that which I think impossible" and since this reaction is the very one that Pyrocles desires. But, taken in another light, the fact that Philoclea can rationalize as she does provides moral commentary on Gynecia's behavior. Gynecia's proposed adultery serves as an example to her daughter and thus is immoral not merely in itself but in its potential consequences. This judgment remains valid even though "Zelmane's" sex frees Philoclea from culpability.

The sense of the process of time in the description of

Philoclea's falling in love is reinforced when she retracts the
vow of chastity written "a few days before Zelmane's coming
. . . as a testimony of her mind, against the suspicion her captivity made her think she lived in" (I, 172). The vow itself
was written on "a goodly white marble stone, that should
seem had been dedicated in ancient time to the Sylvan gods"
(I, 172) and begins with an invocation to the powers of life:

> You living powers enclosed in stately shrine
> Of growing trees: you rural Gods that wield
> Your scepters here, if to your ears divine
> A voice may come, which troubled soul doth yield:
>   This vow receive, this vow O Gods maintain:
> My virgin life no spotted thought shall stain.
>
>   Thou purest stone, whose pureness doth present
> My purest mind; whose temper hard doth show
> My temp'red heart; by thee my promise sent
> Unto myself let after-livers know.
>   No fancy mine, nor others' wrong suspect
>   Make me, O virtuous shame, thy laws neglect.
>
>   O chastity, the chief of heavenly lights,
> Which mak'st us most immortal shape to wear,
> Hold thou my heart, establish thou my sprites:
> To only thee my constant course I bear.
>   Till spotless soul unto thy bosom fly,
>   Such life to lead, such death I vow to die.
>
>   (I, 172)

Philoclea is embarrassed when, after falling in love with "Zelmane," she sees these verses again and writes a retraction:

>   My words, in hope to blaze my stedfast mind,
> This marble chose, as of like temper known:
> But lo, my words defac'd, my fancies blind,
> Blots to the stone, shames to myself I find:
>   And witness am, how ill agree in one,
>   A woman's hand with constant marble stone.
>   My words full weak, the marble full of might;
> My words in store, the marble all alone;

> My words black ink, the marble kindly white;
> My words unseen, the marble still in sight,
>   May witness bear, how ill agree in one,
>   A woman's hand, with constant marble stone.

(I, 173)

The change in Philoclea's attitudes posited by these two sets of verses is the natural product of the operation of time because a shift in temporal perspective implies a psychological shift in the perceiver. But the nature of Philoclea's changed attitudes must be carefully established, because the shift itself indicates something about both the nature of love in the *Arcadia* and the values of temporal change.

Even though the first poem was composed "against the suspicion her captivity made her think she lived in," the language of the poem clearly rejects more than "An uncouth love, which Nature hateth most" (I, 327). In it, she regards "Chastity, the chief of heavenly lights" as a guide to "My virgin life" and so seems to equate chastity and virginity. The psychological foundations for this simplistic attitude are laid in her own innocence. Prior to Pyrocles' arrival, "The sweet-minded Philoclea was in their degree of well-doing, to whom the not knowing of evil serveth for a ground of virtue . . . " (I, 169), and therefore " . . . she was like a young fawn, who coming in the wind of the hunters, doth not know whether it be a thing or no to be eschewed . . . " (I, 169).[10] But the equation of chastity and virginity renders impossible the concept of the chaste wife who enjoys married sex. This runs contrary, as the Hallers point out,[11] to the prevailing Renaissance concept of chastity, which has, perhaps, its fullest expression in Books III and IV of *The Faerie Queene.*[12] The equation, then, is particularly naive since it seems to rule out entirely the possibility of chaste sexual love. There is little reason to suspect, however, that Philoclea had fully worked out the implications of her own vow; a more reasonable assumption is that her youth and innocence, coupled with her rejection of the oracle, have led her to a more extreme position than she might otherwise have taken. In any case, the two poems taken together mark a kind of transition from innocence to experience and suggest that, to a great extent, Philoclea's confusion is a natural consequence of growing up and having to frame "out of her own will the forechoosing of anything" (I, 169)[13]

The first poem, moreover, indicates that Philoclea's equation of virginity and chastity is naive in a temporal sense. Virginity is a static state; it denies process and as Parolles sophistically tells Helena, "There's little can be said in 't; 'tis against the rule of nature" (*All's Well that Ends Well*, I, i, 147). The invocation of the vow directs the audience's attention to Philoclea's naiveté and suggests the self-contained contradiction of the vow itself.

> You living powers enclosed in stately shrine
> Of growing trees: you rural Gods that wield
> Your scepters here . . .

are the powers of life and of growth. And the marble on which the vow is written "had been dedicated in ancient time to the Sylvan gods," gods with whom are identified the processes of procreation and fecundity. So Philoclea, in making what amounts to a vow of virginity, has called upon the gods to whom virginity is antithetical and has attempted to convert process to stasis. But time cannot be denied and the retraction becomes in order.

But time has not come to a stop and the process is still incomplete. Philoclea cannot understand as the audience does either her place in time or the consequences of having fallen in love. At this point she can only think that the passage of time means inconstancy; this is the effect of the recurring final lines of each stanza of the second poem: " . . . how ill agree in one,/A woman's hand with constant marble stone." Not until Pyrocles reveals himself is a third, unwritten poem possible, wherein Philoclea could celebrate, without shame, the chaste love she feels for the Prince, a love that could include a union of the concepts of mutability and constancy in time. The combination of Philoclea's falling in love, her vow of virginity, and its retraction all undercut a static vision of love and tie the erotic theme to the idea of temporality in Book II.

The opening chapters of Book II, then, do very little to advance the narrative in an obvious way; the sole event, Gynecia's accident, does not become important until later in the book. Nonetheless these chapters convey the important information that Pamela returns Musidorus's love and that Philoclea, although ignorant of her lover's identity or even his sex, is in love with Pyrocles. This information leads the audience to expect a satisfactory conclusion to the suit of the two princes. Finally, the opening chapters establish the temporal emphasis of the book and relate the erotic theme to that emphasis. Musidorus's narration, which is to follow, will serve a similar function for the political theme.

iii

The relationship between Musidorus's narration and the rest of the *Arcadia* has been variously interpreted by Sidney's critics. Edwin Greenlaw, for example, argues that the incidents of Musidorus's narrative are thematically unified "through the fact that the misfortunes which the heroes . . . seek to correct proceed . . . from tyannical or unjust government . . . "[14] Myrick, although he differs from Greenlaw in some respects — notably on the matter of the political emphasis of the *Arcadia* — agrees in principle by emphasizing the didacticism of Sidney's work. "The teaching is especially plain in the narrative of events prior to the main story, where time after time it is made clear by contrast."[15] The idea of the didactic function of Musidorus's narrative and of the whole *Arcadia* is taken up, again with some changes, by Tillyard when he claims that the *Arcadia* is about the education of princes.[16] While it would be difficult, and probably pointless, to deny that the *Arcadia* has a didactic element, this kind of analysis does not differentiate between the main narrative and the delegated narrations; it does not allow for the fact that the primary auditor for the delegated narrations is someone other than the audience.[17] For example, the primary auditor for Musidorus's narration is Pamela, and a discussion of that narration must include Musidorus's reason for telling his early history and the effect of his narration on Pamela, not merely the effect that it has on the audience.

Recent criticism of the *Arcadia* has attempted to account for these factors. Walter Davis ties the knot between Musidorus's narrative and the whole of the *Arcadia* thematically when he argues that each section in Musidorus's narration "is about civil strife, usually a result of Passion overpowering Reason."[18] But the relationship Davis suggests depends on his neoplatonic reading of the *Arcadia*, and that reading is certainly doubtful.[19] Rodney Delasanta relates Musidorus's narration to Musidorus's character when he points out that the narration from shipwreck to the restoration of Leonatus to the throne of Paphlagonia is marked by the singular absence of female characters. According to Delasanta, then, "Musidorus' narration . . . tends to dramatize 'merely masculine prowess.' "[20] Stimulating though this conception may be, however, it does not clearly establish a relationship between the matter of Musidorus's narrative with the matter of the main narrative, which is Nancy Rothwax Lindheim's concern. She claims that underlying the rhetoric of Musidorus's narration is his need to establish his claim to nobility. "Thus, it is not surprising that his stories should illustrate the art of good government, the nature of a princely education, acts of public chivalry and the noble virtues of friendship, magnanimity and justice."[21] Although Lindheim's analysis is perceptive and hard to fault, it neglects the temporal aspect of Musidorus's narrative.

Musidorus begins his narrative with a description of his uncle and Pyrocles' father, Euarchus, who stands in the *Arcadia* as the paradigm of the ideal prince.

Who as he was most wise to see what was best, and most just in the

performing what he saw, and temperate in abstaining from anything
anyway contrary: so think I, no thought can imagine a greater heart
to see and contemn danger, where danger would offer to make any
wrongful threatening upon him. A prince, that indeed especially
measured his greatness by his goodness: and if for anything he loved
greatness, it was, because therein he might exercise his goodness. A
prince of a goodly aspect, and the more goodly by a grave majesty,
wherewith his mind did deck his outward graces; strong of body,
and so much the stronger, as he by a well-disciplined exercise taught
it both to do, and suffer. (I, 185)

After giving this account of Euarchus, Musidorus describes his
reign, which, like the king himself, is a model of good government: "In sum (peerless princess) I might as easily set down
the whole art of government, as to lay before your eyes the
picture of his proceedings" (I, 187). Clearly the bad kings of
Phrygia and Pontus and the "*Paphlagonian* unkind King,"
whose stories will follow, are to be tested against this model.
In an indirect comment on Basilius, Musidorus suggests that
the limitations of the ruler of Arcadia brought forth in Book I
are not unavoidable — the ideal king is possible in fact as well
as in theory. The description of Euarchus also indicates that
the emphasis has shifted from the erotic theme of the first
portion of Book II to the second theme, the political. Finally,
the last sentence in the passage cited above justifies Musidorus's relating his and Pyrocles' education, for it clearly
indicates a causal relationship between nurture and nature,
between past training and present behavior.

The sense of the importance of causality manifested
through time is also apparent in the events heralding the
birth of Pyrocles. Soothsayers at Musidorus's birth "affirmed
strange and incredible things should be performed by that
child" (I, 188). As a result of predictions " . . . the King of
Phrygia (who oversuperstitiously thought himself touched
in the matter) sought by force to destroy the infant, to prevent his after-expectations . . . " (I, 188).[22] When Musidorus's
father, Dorilaus, is attacked, Euarchus, who is his wife's
brother, comes to his defense. In consequence of this action
Euarchus marries Dorilaus's sister, and the product of this

marriage is Pyrocles. Thus the sequence of events beginning with the birth of Musidorus leads directly in a causal way to the birth of Pyrocles.

The war between Euarchus and Phrygia indirectly aids Pyrocles and Musidorus after the first shipwreck. In order to escape drowning as their ship broke up, Musidorus explains, the two princes "leaped to a rib of the ship, which broken from his fellows, floated with more likelihood to do service, than any other limb of that ruinous body . . ." (I, 194). But the rib was already occupied by two brothers, Leucippus and Nelsus, and the weight of the four men threatened to drag it under. The two brothers, in order to save the princes' lives "willingly left hold of the board, committing themselves to the sea's rage, and even when they meant to die, themselves praying for the princes' lives" (I, 194). Of the most immediate importance is the reason for the brothers' sacrifice, which is carefully established by Musidorus. During the war waged by Phrygia on Thessalia after the birth of Musidorus, Leucippus and Nelsus had been captured and sold to yet a third country to be held for ransom. But because the figure demanded was excessive, their friends and relatives had been unable to pay for their release and they remained incarcerated for thirteen years while Pyrocles and Musidorus grew to young manhood. Hearing of the plight of Leucippus and Nelsus, the young Princes sold their jewels and otherwise indebted themselves in order to pay the brothers' ransom. Thus the brothers' sacrifice pays a moral debt incurred some years earlier and just as the Phrygian war is the initial point in the causal chain leading to Pyrocles' birth, it is also the initial point in the causal chain leading to the sacrifice of Leucippus and Nelsus. These two apparently independent episodes, then, have the same first cause and this implies not only that causal chains are significant in themselves but that such chains extend far beyond the immediate moment.

Clearly, however, the causal chains leading to the birth of Pyrocles and to the sacrifice of the brothers are fairly simple and straightforward. But they take on added complexity as Musidorus's narrative proceeds. When Pyrocles lands in Phrygia,[23] the king of that country immediately plans his execution. The execution is stayed only to exchange Pyrocles for Musidorus, who in turn is saved by Pyrocles, who had disguised himself as a servant to the executioner, "a far notabler proof of his friendship, considering the height of his mind, than any death could be" (I, 199), for the purpose. The roots of these threats to the lives of the princes lie in the prophecy made at Musidorus's birth — the same prophecy that had earlier caused Phrygia to invade Thessalia. Moreover, the princes' involvement in the affairs of Pontus is tied to the sacrifice made by Leucippus and Nelsus, for these noble kinsmen "drowned . . . were not, but got with painful swimming upon a rock: from whence (after being come as near famishing, as before drowning) the weather breaking up, they were brought to the mainland of Pontus . . . " (I, 202). The King of Pontus, acting on his counselor's advice, first takes on the brothers as trusted courtiers, but then suddenly turns "(and every turn with him was a downfall) to lock them up in prison . . . " (I, 203). When Pyrocles and Musidorus ask for their servants' liberty, the King "caused their heads to be stricken off . . . and sent them with unroyal reproaches to Musidorus and Pyrocles . . . " (I, 203-4). In retaliation, the princes gather forces in Phrygia "(a kingdom wholly at their commandment, by the love of the people, and gratefulness of the [new] king," (I, 204), enter Pontus, and depose the unjust ruler. Thus, the deposition of the King of Pontus rests on the initial sacrifice of Leucippus and Nelsus as well as on the preceding deposition of the King of Phrygia. Quite clearly, then, the causal chains, temporal markers, involved in this comparatively simple sequence of events interrelate the events.

The events themselves are political in their emphasis. The Kings of Phrygia and of Pontus are set forth as models of bad kings. Phrygia is an example of the suspicious king, "a prince of a melancholy constitution both of body and mind; wickedly sad, ever musing of horrible matters; suspecting, or rather condemning all men of evil, because his mind had no eye to espy goodness . . . " (I, 196). The effect of such a ruler as Phrygia is borne by the populace and the reign is one of fear and cruelty. "So as servitude came mainly upon that poor people . . . while suspicion bred the mind of cruelty, and the effects of cruelty stirred a new cause of suspicion" (I, 197). Both the man and his reign are in clear contrast to Euarchus and his reign described earlier. The political lesson implicit in the earlier description, then, is being reinforced by the negative *exemplum* of Phrygia.

Similarly, the description of the King of Pontus is in marked contrast to that of Euarchus. But Pontus is a tyrant "not through suspicion, greediness, or revengefulness, as he of Phrygia, but (as I may term it) of a wanton cruelty . . . " (I, 202). The signal characteristic of Pontus's malignancy is his inconstancy; he rules by caprice, "giving sometimes prodigally, not because he loved them to whom he gave, but because he lusted to give: punishing, not so much for hate or anger, as because he felt not the smart of punishment . . . " (I, 202). This rule by whim leads to disorder in the kingdom and to the advance in the court of "a man of the most envious disposition, that (I think) ever infected the air with his breath . . . " (I, 203). In the description of Euarchus, as Lindheim points out,[24] two vices are mentioned as specifically absent from the character of the ideal prince: suspicion and envy. The first of these is the King of Phrygia's most notable characteristic and the second can be seen in the King of Pontus's chief counselor, "a man of the most envious disposition" who, along with the King's "wanton cruelty," establishes the framework for behavior in Pontus. The stories of these three men, then, provide a political lesson for the audience at the same time as they show Pamela, the primary auditor of the stories, Musidorus's nobility. Finally, the three stories intertwine the political theme of the *Arcadia* with the temporal emphasis of the second book.

iv

The last section of Musidorus's narrative is set apart in tone and matter from the material that precedes it, as his prefatory remark makes clear:

> For scarcely were they [Pyrocles and Musidorus] out of the confines of Pontus, but that as they rode alone armed (for alone they went, one serving the other) they met an adventure; which though not so notable for any great effect they performed, yet worthy to be remembered for the unused examples therein, as well of true natural goodness, as of wretched ungratefulness. (I, 206)

It would be unwise to overemphasize the differentiation between the tale of the Paphlagonian King and, for example, the tales of the Kings of Phrygia and Pontus. Such an overemphasis leads in one direction to neglect of the didactic aspect of the earlier episodes and in the other direction to neglect of the integral role played by this episode in what is to come. Nevertheless, a difference has to be noted. The opening sentence of the episode carries with it a sense of beginning and one of the few nonpastoral seasonal references in the *Arcadia*.

> It was in the kingdom of Galatia,[25] the season being (as in the depth of winter) very cold, and as then suddenly grown to so extreme and foul a storm, that never any winter (I think) brought forth a fouler child: so that the princes were even compelled by the hail, that the pride of the wind blew into their faces, to seek some shrouding place which a certain hollow rock offering unto them, they made it their shield against the tempest's fury. (I, 206-7)

The device of the storm is, of course, a fairly standard romance motif presaging some fundamental change of state. As such, this storm anticipates the storms in Shakespeare's last plays — *Pericles* (III, i), *The Winter's Tale* (III, iii), and *The Tempest* (I, i) — and might have the same kind of impact on the audience as the description of winter in *Sir Gawain and the Green Knight* (ll. 726-39). But the transition marked here differs in kind from the sorts of transitions found in the more traditional romances: from this point to the close of Book II the princes' adventures will lose some of the trappings of the older form at least in the sense that they take on greater complexity of choice.[26] Moreover, the characters in "the story of the *Paphlagonian* unkind King," particularly Plexirtus, play important roles in the narrative delegated to Pyrocles, and this episode, therefore, lays the groundwork for a new temporal-causal sequence to follow later.

The story of the Paphlagonian King and his two sons is a familiar one because, as has been long recognized, it is the source of the Gloucester subplot in *King Lear*. This means that it has been subject to more detailed scrutiny, perhaps, than any other single section of the *Arcadia*.[27] Even so, criticism of this episode has, for the most part, neglected its relationship with other portions of the *Arcadia*, overemphasized its didactic component, and ignored its density and complexity. In summary form, the story of the Paphlagonian King is as follows: Taking refuge from a storm, Pyrocles and Musidorus overhear an aged man and his son exchange complaints, the elder wishing to die and the younger trying to prevent him. The two princes intervene and are told, in the greatest detail by the elder, that the old man is the King of Paphlagonia, who has two sons, one legitimate and the other a bastard. Persuaded by Plexirtus, the bastard, that Leonatus, the legitimate, wants to usurp the throne before the death of his father, the old King has tried to have Leonatus killed by some of his servants. "But those thieves (better natured to my son than myself) spared his life, letting him go, to learn to live poorly: which he did, giving himself to be a private soldier, in a country hereby"[28] (I, 209). Once rid of the threat of Leonatus, Plexirtus has craftily taken over the kingdom from his father and has had the old

King blinded. Because Plexirtus has prohibited the Paphla-
gonians from aiding the blind King, and in remorse for his
bad judgment, the old man attempted suicide, but was
thwarted by Leonatus. Upon the completion of this "matter
in itself lamentable, lamentably expressed by the old prince"
(I, 210), Plexirtus arrives with forty men "only of purpose to
murder this brother . . . " (I, 210). The defenders are aided
by the arrival of the King of Pontus, who "having had a
dream which had fixed his imagination vehemently upon
some great danger, presently to follow those two princes
whom he most dearly loved . . . " (I, 211), manages to turn
the tide of the conflict. Plexirtus, in turn, is joined by the
forces of Tydeus and Telenor and so escapes death. As Leonatus is crowned king by his father, who dies "his heart
broken with unkindness and affliction, stretched so far beyond his limits with this excess of comfort, as it was able no
longer to keep safe his vital spirits" (I, 212), Pyrocles and
Musidorus raise forces in Phrygia and Pontus and lay siege
to Plexirtus. Upon discovering that force will not avail him,
Plexirtus cunningly feigns repentance and is reunited with
his brother. Pyrocles and Musidorus, having apparently
settled the situation, leave with Tydeus and Telenor to come
to the aid of Erona, and Musidorus's narrative breaks off as
Tydeus and Telenor are recalled by Plexirtus "to advance a
conquest he was about" (I, 214).

The most immediately obvious fact to be noted about this
episode is that it is not end-stopped as the two preceding episodes apparently were. Although the rightful king has been
established on the throne of Paphlagonia much as good kings
have taken over Phrygia and Pontus, the usurper is left alive
at the end of this episode. Yet, in describing the confession
Plexirtus uses to effect the reconciliation, Musidorus implies
that the bastard retains his evil nature.

Where what submission he [Plexirtus] used, how cunningly in making
greater the fault he made the faultiness the less, how artificially he
could set out the torments of his own conscience, with the burden-

some cumber he had found of his ambitious desires, how finely seeming to desire nothing but death, as ashamed to live, he begged life, in the refusing it, I am not cunning enough to be able to express. (I, 213)

The central words here emphasize the manner of Plexirtus's confession rather than its matter; the confession is made "cunningly," "artificially," and "finely seeming." Obviously, then, the evil effects of Plexirtus's villainous nature will not cease with this episode. Finally, the fact that the story of the Paphlagonian King is presented in retrospective narrative confirms at the moment Musidorus's implication. Thus the story of the Paphlagonian King serves to arouse expectations in the audience concerning future episodes in the *Arcadia*.

Despite Musidorus's introductory comment, the didacticism of this episode is surely less clear-cut and perhaps less overt than the didacticism of the Phrygia and Pontus episodes. If the source of civil disorder in Phrygia and Pontus can be centered in the tyrants ruling those countries, whose evil nature can be easily determined, the source of dissolution in Paphlagonia is more diffuse. On the one hand, the vortex of the evil is surely the usurping Plexirtus; but, on the other hand, that evil is allowed to gain power because of the serious misjudgments of the old king.[29] The increase in ethical complexity in the Paphlagonian episode results at least partly from the diffusion of the causes of political evil and tends to humanize the traditional romance. The Kings of Phrygia and Pontus both have the status of the dragon in a folk tale of slaying the dragon; they operate independently of human weakness in causing human misery and hence seem almost preternatural in their malevolence. Once they are slain the state can be put back in order. The Paphlagonian episode also has its "dragon," Plexirtus, but here the force of evil has efficacy only because of peculiarly human weaknesses of the other characters, especially the old King. Evil in the *Arcadia*, then, though inescapably present, has power only because men either cannot recognize it or cannot cope with its operation.

This sense that human weakness and moral complexity is at the center of the Paphlagonian episode is reinforced by the description of Tydeus and Telenor. Like Phalantus in Book I, Tydeus and Telenor are, at least potentially, virtuous men. Like him, they commit their vicious acts because of a commitment to an abstract moral code, in this instance the friendship code, " . . . so as though they did not like the evil he did, yet they liked him that did the evil . . . " (I, 211-12). This is summed up when Musidorus says that Tydeus and Telenor "(willingly hoodwinking themselves from seeing his [Plexirtus's] faults, and binding themselves to believe what he said) often abused the virtue of courage to defend his foul vice of injustice" (I, 214). The disastrous consequences to which this virtuous commitment to vice can ultimately lead include the becoming vicious or evil of the virtuous characters themselves. This is established in the earlier tale of the two giant brothers of Pontus. They had been superb servants to the King of Pontus, especially in military matters, until he whimsically dismissed them from service. Because the dismissal grew not out of merit but out of caprice, the brothers became choleric and ravaged the countryside,

> so that where in the time that they obeyed a master, their anger was a serviceable power of the mind to do public good; so now unbridled, and blind judge of itself, it made wickedness violent, and praised itself in excellency of mischief; almost to the ruin of the country, not greatly regarded by their careless and loveless king. (I, 205)

The misbehavior of the two giants shows how decent men can become totally corrupted; it leads the audience to anticipate the different, though analogous, disaster awaiting Tydeus and Telenor at the hands of Plexirtus. Clearly the story argues that a ruler is obligated to his servants and is responsible for controlling them. In reminding the audience that military forces can run amuck, the story of the two giants reinforces the negative *exemplum* of the King of Pontus.

The Paphlagonian episode, illustrating human weakness, is a commentary on events in the main plot. Basilius's withdrawal from his responsibility as a ruler results from his personal weakness, especially his folly in trying to circumvent the oracle. Among the results of this retreat from royal responsibility will be the rebellion sponsored by Cecropia, who, like Plexirtus, is fundamentally evil. It is not enough to conclude that Basilus's political difficulties stem primarily from a source of evil outside himself: the Paphlagonian sequence shows that such problems arise when human weakness leads rulers to faulty judgments. Human weakness renders men unable to cope with evil, and may give rise to situations in which evil can flourish. This sequence not only points out Basilius's responsibility in the Arcadian uprising but, by showing that such weakness is only human, prevents us from condemning him unduly.

The events in the Paphlagonian episode are more complex than those in the preceding episodes of Musidorus's narrative. A similar complexity will characterize the stories of Plangus and Erona later in the *Arcadia*, and also the narrative delegated to Pyrocles. The Paphlagonian story involves more persons than the preceding episodes. Besides Pyrocles, Musidorus, and the royal family, the cast of characters includes the new Kings of Pontus and Phrygia as well as Tydeus and Telenor. And these characters interact in complex ways; Pontus and the brothers aid the princes and Plexirtus respectively; the forces gathered in Phrygia and Pontus enable Pyrocles and Musidorus to besiege Plexirtus's castle. In short, the Paphlagonian episode has more immediately expansive and inclusive effects than the earlier episodes do; causal chains have moved significantly outward and will continue to do so, compelling the princes to make increasingly more complex ethical choices while reducing the absoluteness of those choices.[30] The audience recognizes the ambivalence inherent in real-life situations, a perception different from any evoked by the traditional romance or by narratives solely informed by such ethical systems as Ficino's Neoplatonism. This effect, coupled with the internalization of the audience, produces the sensation of experiencing events in time.

v

Musidorus is about to go on with the further adventures of

himself and Pyrocles as they attempted to rescue Erona, Queen of Lycia. Then Pamela interrupts, saying, "I have heard . . . that part of the story of Plangus when he passed through this country: therefore you may (if you list) pass over that war of Erona's quarrel . . . " (I, 214). Although Musidorus tries to use the respite to court Pamela, she awakens Mopsa and both courting and story-telling are discontinued for a while. The ensuing pastoral interlude of bathing in the river Ladon is marked by two events, one entirely comic and the other potentially serious.

After lunch, Philoclea and Pamela decide to refresh themselves in the river, partly because such is "the manner of the Arcadian nymphs" (I, 215), partly to avoid the heat of the day, and partly to escape the tedium of Miso's conversation. Pyrocles sees them leave the lodge and follows, not knowing they are on their way to bathe. They stop to watch a water spaniel frolic in the river for a few moments until, emerging, he loses himself in the weeds. Pyrocles elects not to swim but watches the ladies undress themselves. His reason for not joining them in their bath is obvious — he cannot expose himself as a man — and his situation at this point is a comic highlight of his disguise. In fact, Pyrocles almost loses control of himself during what is tantamount to a striptease.

> Zelmane would have put to her helping hand, but she was taken with such a quivering, that she thought it more wisdom to lean herself to a tree and look on, while Miso amd Mopsa (like a couple of foreswat melters) were getting the pure silver of their bodies out of the ore of their garments. But as the raiments went off to receive kisses of the ground, Zelmane envied the happiness of all, but of the smock was even jealous, and when that was taken away too, and that Philoclea remained (for her Zelmane only marked) like a diamond taken from out the rock, or rather like the sun getting from under a cloud, and showing his naked beams to the full view, then was the beauty too much for a patient sight, the delight too strong for a stayed conceit: so that Zelmane could not choose but run, to touch, embrace and kiss her. But conscience made her come to herself, and leave Philoclea, who blushing, and withal smiling, making shamefastness pleasant, and pleasure shamefast, tenderly moved her feet,

unwonted to feel the naked ground, till the touch of the cold water
made a pretty kind of shrugging come over her body, like the
twinkling of the fairest among the fixed stars. (I, 217)

The humor of this picture is at Pyrocles' and Philoclea's
expense: "Zelmane" is a man, with whom Philoclea is in love.
The effect of the laughter caused by the humor is, of course,
comic or satiric distance and the externalization of the audience. But this effect is undercut by the second function of
the scene — to let Pyrocles see Philoclea in the nude. The
pleasure he takes in the sight — "What tongue can her perfections tell" — is shared directly by at least the masculine
members of the audience — "wee are ravished with delight to
see a faire woman" (III, 40). The audience at least takes
pleasure in the fact that Pyrocles enjoys the sight of Philoclea. Since looking at naked ladies is a taboo "wish," the
comic distance imposed on this scene serves as the "defense"
structure that enables the audience to enjoy the sight as
well.[31] In any case, the comic distancing and pleasurable
internalization illustrate the control of polarization also
found, for example, in the *Arcadia*'s presentation of love.
This scene, moreover, is one of those which break up the
retrospective narratives and keep the audience interested in
the love affairs in progress.

As Pyrocles, "whose sight [of Philoclea] was gainsaid by
nothing but the transparent veil of Ladon" (I, 218), stands
watching his beloved bathe, the water spaniel observed earlier
returns to steal first Philoclea's glove and then "a little book
of four or five leaves of paper . . . " (I, 222). Not knowing
whether the book has any importance, Pyrocles follows the
dog and sees it deliver the book "to a gentleman who secretly
lay there" (I, 222). Demanding the return of glove and book,
Pyrocles discovers that this "gentleman" is a rival for Philoclea's love. Enraged, Pyrocles attempts to force the stranger
into combat but the latter refuses, "saying withal, 'God
forbid I should use my sword against you, since (if I be not
deceived) you are the same famous Amazon, that both defended my lady's just title of beauty against the valiant

Phalantus, and saved her life in killing the lion . . .' " (I, 223). But Pyrocles persists and the "gentleman" must put up a stout defense. Finally, having wounded his opponent in the thigh, Pyrocles comes to his senses and stops the attack. Unwilling, however, to forgive the unintended rivalry, he warns Amphialus that " '. . . you shall meet with a near kinsman of mine, Pyrocles Prince of Macedon, and I give you my word, he for me shall maintain this quarrel against you' " (I, 224).

This clash between Pyrocles and the stranger of course recalls the earlier duel between Philoxenus and Amphialus (I, 70-71); in both cases one party tries to avoid conflict and indeed does not even know the cause of the trouble. The parallelism, moreover, is reinforced by the fact that the "gentleman" turns out to be Amphialus and the mischievous water spaniel the dog that was said to be his sole companion during his self-imposed exile. Although Pyrocles is among the best and most virtuous of men, he is not immune to the disruptive power of love; like the other characters in the *Arcadia*, he is subject to the irrationality that love can occasion. This likens him to Philoxenus earlier and Amphialus later and suggests that only his greater self-control, his greater self-awareness, enables him to avoid such catastrophes as those characters experience. The contrast between them and Pyrocles enables us to repudiate the charge that Pyrocles is an unthinking slave to passion. At the same time, his passionate love prevents us from suspecting that he is a kind of erotic Talus.

In this sequence, moreoever, Sidney uses implicit comedy, more subtle perhaps than in the bathing scene, to modulate the audience's response. There is some absurdity in the second apparently unprovoked assault on Amphialus by one he does not wish to fight, and although he is not a comic figure in himself, like Anaxius on the chivalric level or Dametas on the pastoral level, the situations in which he finds himself become comic by repetition. In short, then, this episode embodies a serious criticism of the effects of love, but this criticism is extenuated by subtle comedy. And so, despite the irrationality of Pyrocles' action, the audience remains internalized. Finally, this sequence picks up the story left incomplete by Helen in Book I. It thus provides a temporal connection between a retrospective narrative in that book and the main plot as it continues in Book II and is the first of many such connections. Such a relationship between an earlier retrospective narrative and present events shows how the past has a bearing on the present, which is the apex of a pyramid.

After Amphialus's wound is treated and he departs, Pyrocles and the ladies examine the little book that the spaniel had stolen. It contains verses by Basilius — a dialogue between him and Plangus. These serve as modulation into Philoclea's and Pamela's narratives concerning Erona and Plangus. Rodney Delasanta suggests that this modulation is poorly handled and is "disproportionate in length even to the structural importance of the Plangus-Erona episode."[32] The difficulty here is that the sequence to which Delasanta refers is multifunctional — not, as he implies, solely a modulation between narratives. The fight with Amphialus has shown the power of love over Pyrocles and has tied the main plot to Helen's retrospective narrative. The lesser poetic quality of Basilius's dialogue and the role he ascribes to himself there are commentary on his self-image. His relative ineptitude at poetic composition contrasts unfavorably with the talents of the princes and princesses and shows his limitations; in the *Arcadia* poetic ability and aptitude for story-telling are directly related to the moral stature of the poet. Basilius's self-image in the dialogue parallels the role played by Lady Philosophy in Boethius's *Consolation of Philosophy* and clearly contrasts with his actions in the main plot. Finally, Plangus's part in the dialogue emphasizes his response to the threatened death of Erona. This anticipates the ambivalent response of Erona to the threatened death of Antiphilus in the narrative delegated to Philoclea.

The tales of Erona and of Plangus introduced by the verse dialogue and interrupted by Miso's insistence that everybody be allowed to tell tales clearly parallel each other and, in a sense, sum up the action in the other tales. Davis argues, for example, that Sidney's placing the "Plangus-Erona tragedy" in the center of Book II allows him to bring together threads of the other retrospective narratives, and that the "Plangus-Erona tragedy" marks a clear dividing line between the stories told by Musidorus and those told by Pyrocles. Davis makes a dubious distinction between the outer workings of "passion overpowering reason" and "the inner workings of passion in a character rather than its effects in deeds."[33] But the two tales continue the transition noted earlier in the episode of the Paphlagonian King in narrative and moral situation. Again, although Davis implies that it occurs in the center of Book II, the verse dialogue barely suggests the tragic component of the Plangus-Erona story, and the tragedy does not become manifest until Basilius's narrative at the end of the book. The lag, incidentally, between the beginning of the Plangus-Erona story by Philoclea and Pamela and its continuation by Basilius almost a hundred pages later contributes to the audience's sense of the importance and complexity of temporal process.

The interrelatedness of the two parts of the Plangus-Erona story is further indicated by the parallels between them. Each begins with a crime against love. Erona, having sacrilegiously destroyed all the images of Cupid in Lycia, is punished by the mischievous god. The device is, of course, a familiar one in both folk tales and in literature; Chaucer's Troilus, for example, commits just such a sin and must therefore fall in love with Criseyde.[34] The punishment of the infidel sometimes shows the irresistible power of love, as it does here. Plangus's offense against love differs from Erona's; instead of denying love's power, he mistakes lust for love and so commits adultery. As Pamela relates the beginning of Plangus's story, she questions whether his emotion "may be called love, which he rather did take into himself willingly, than by which he was taken forcibly" (I, 243). Her distinction between lust as an act of the will and love as a force outside the self explains the complaints made earlier by Pyrocles and

Musidorus as each finds himself in love. These complaints turn not on a sense that love is sinful — for the erotic drive when sinful turns out to be lust — but on a sense of the restriction that love places on the self. With awareness of love's power comes an awareness that the individual cannot impose his own values on the world. The princes' love complaints therefore show — in a comic way — the limitations of the self, besides expressing regret for their lost sense of freedom. Plangus's lust for Andromana recalls Phalantus's affectation for Artesia in Book I and the serious consequences of his behavior. His alienation from his father, his step-mother's attempt to have him murdered, and the antipathy that develops between Iberia and Armenia all point to the kind of personal and political disasters that can result from mistaken love or lust. The two stories are also parallel in the way each ends at the point where Antiphilus has been redeemed by the two princes, Tiridates killed, and Artaxia placed on the throne of Armenia.

To Pyrocles, the primary auditor of the stories of Erona and Plangus, the two stories do not convey any new information, because, although the princesses are unaware of the fact, he was a participant in the adventures described. His curiosity had been piqued by "the speech of Erona's death" (I, 231) in the verse dialogue, but the narration of that matter is delayed by Basilius's arrival. Therefore these narratives function differently from Musidorus's narrative, which had the internal purpose of informing Pamela of Musidorus's noble state. Nevertheless, the stories narrated by the two princesses do reflect the tellers. Philoclea's tale deals with a woman, Pamela's with a man, and this tends to substantiate Danby's point that of the two Philoclea is the more purely feminine.[3][5] Far more important, however, is the similarity of Erona's plight to Philoclea's own. Just as Erona committed sacrilege against Cupid, so too had Philoclea made her vow of chastity; and just as Erona was punished by falling in love with an unworthy man, so Philoclea has fallen in love with "Zelmane."

Miso's interruption, which separates the story of Erona

from that of Plangus, serves a double function in terms of the narrative that surrounds it: Miso's mistaking of Pan for Cupid is a commentary on love, and Mopsa's tale is a commentary on the narrative technique of the *Arcadia*. Miso learned about Cupid from a "good old woman . . . (O the good wold woman, well may the bones rest of the good wold woman)" (I, 238) and therefore describes him grotesquely in her anti-love poem, "Poor Painters oft with silly Poets join,"

> Yet bears he still his parent's stately gifts,
> A horned head, cloven feet, and thousand eyes,
> Some gazing still, some winking wily shifts,
> With long large ears where never rumor dies.
>> His horned head doth seem the heaven to spite:
>> His cloven foot doth never tread aright.
>
> Thus half a man, with man he daily haunts,
> Cloth'd in the shape which soonest may deceive:
> Thus half a beast, each beastly vice he plants,
> In those weak hearts that his advice receive.

> (I, 240)

Davis is surely right in claiming that part of the humor here stems from Miso's mistake in identities[36] and part from the advice given by the "good old woman" to "do what thou list with all those fellows, one after another; and it recks not much what they do to thee, so it be in secret; but upon my charge, never love none of them" (I, 238-39). He is also right in noticing that "the moral of this interlude is clear: love is what you make it, a beast to the whore, a god to the gentle."[37] But his Neoplatonic extension contrasting *amor ferinus* and Heavenly Love with its either-or implication is as suspect as the rest of his attempt to impose Ficino on Sidney.

Davis misses another aspect of comic irony, namely, that Pan is the tutelary god of Arcadia. This fact aligns fecundity with love and so suggests that love involves a physical process as well as psychological and moral ones. But Miso would deny this connection just as she seems to have accepted fully the old woman's advice to "never love none of them." The denial would, if generally accepted, put a stop to the life processes, as is indicated in the portrait of Cupid-Pan:

> This monster sat like a hangman upon a pair of gallows, in his right hand he was painted holding a crown of laurel, in his left hand a purse of money, and out of his mouth hung a lace of two fair pictures, of a man and a woman, and such a countenance he showed, as if he would persuade folks by those allurements to come thither and be hanged. (I, 238)

Implicit in this portrait is the equivalence of Cupid-Pan's manifestation in the world, poetry (the "crown of laurel") and money. Art and sexuality are prostituted as they are in the fact that the poem and painting are a return "for a little pleasure." This irony undermines the values in both and makes it impossible for the audience to take either seriously.

Just as Miso's description of Cupid-Pan is a comic and self-reflexive commentary on love and sexuality that may put the loves of Erona and Plangus into a new perspective, so Mopsa's abortive attempt at tale-telling changes our perspective on the narrative techniques of Musidorus, Philoclea, Pamela, *et al.*, as well as that of the *Arcadia* as a whole. Davis identifies Mopsa's partial narrative as "a silly medieval tale,"[38] and it is certainly a compendium of motifs from folk tales and traditional romances. It includes a king's daughter, a magic knight who disappears when the princess asks the forbidden question, a journey through a "cruel wilderness, as dark as pitch" (I, 241), and magic nuts that are not to be opened "till she was come to the extremest misery that ever tongue could speak of" (I, 241). The tale is informed by a naive temporal progression that may be seen in the following:

> So one day, as his daughter was sitting in her window, playing upon a harp, as sweet as any rose; and combing her head with a comb all of precious stones, there came in a knight into the court, upon a goodly horse, one hair of gold, and the other of silver; *and so* the knight casting up his eyes to the window, did fall into such love with

her, that he grew not worth the bread he eat . . . *And so in May, when all true hearts rejoice*, they stole out of the castle, without staying so much as for their breakfast. (I, 241)

Mopsa's attempt at narrative is blissfully interrupted just as Chaucer's *Tale of Sir Thopas* is interrupted in a similar situation. In both content and form, it contrasts with the narratives included within the *Arcadia* and with the techniques manifested in the work as a whole. The contrast, moreover, tends to emphasize the complexity and sophistication of the whole; since Miso's interruption is anti-sexual and Mopsa's tale is romantic in a simplistic sense, neither the view of Miso nor Mopsa concerning love seems adequate to explain the attitudes toward love in the *Arcadia*.

The sequence beginning with the bathing scene and ending with Pamela's tale of Plangus, then, is multifunctional. The parallel tales of Erona and Plangus start causal chains that are to continue through the narratives delegated to Pyrocles and Basilius. With the story of the Paphlagonian King, they suggest the princes' inability to settle complicated moral problems; so, too, they suggest the inadvisability of viewing the *Arcadia* as a moral treatise. Through the war waged by Tiridates for Erona, the parallel tales also demonstrate the interrelatedness of the erotic and political themes within the temporal emphasis of Book II. The conflict between Amphialus and Pyrocles, which precedes the tales of Erona and Plangus, not only relates the main plot to Helen's retrospective narrative in Book I, but shows the power of love over such an estimable character as Pyrocles. But the light comic touch in the sequence, as well as Miso's comic confusion of Pan and Cupid, prevents us from taking as fundamental to the *Arcadia* a negative attitude toward love — the kind of attitude implicit in the Pyrocles-Amphialus conflict and in Miso's antieroticism. Finally, the contrast between Mopsa's narrative and the rest of the *Arcadia* shows how Sidney's narrative has moved away from the simplistic world views of traditional narratives and toward what, for want of a better word, may be called realistic.

vi

The set of attitudes toward love expressed in the preceding sequence prepares us for Pyrocles' narrative that is to come. After interrupting Pamela's narrative of Plangus, Basilius takes Pyrocles to visit the injured Gynecia. The two lusting parents make Pyrocles feel " . . . like the poor child, whose father while he beats him, will make him believe it is for love; or like the sick man, to whom the physician swears, the ill-tasting wallowish medicine he proffers, is of a good taste . . . " (I, 251). Clearly the passion offered by both Gynecia and Basilius is not radically distinct in kind from that to which Miso was referring in her interruption. Pyrocles is himself aware of a distinction between love and lust, as in the verses he composes after escaping Gynecia and Basilius for a moment.

> Loved I am, and yet complain of love:
> As loving not, accus'd in Love I die.
> When pity most I crave, I cruel prove:
> Still seeking Love, love found as much I fly.
>   Burnt in myself, I muse at others' fire:
> What I call wrong, I do the same, and more:
> Barr'd of my will, I have beyond desire:
> I wail for want, and yet am chok'd with store.
>
>   This is thy work, thou god for ever blind:
> Though thousands old, a boy entit'led still.
> Thus children do the silly birds they find,
> With stroking hurt, and too much cramming kill.
>   Yet thus much Love, O Love, I crave of thee:
> Let me be Lov'd, or else not loved be.   (I, 253)

This complaint distinguishes implicitly between the lust of both Gynecia and Basilius and the love Pyrocles seeks with Philoclea.

The distinction between the merely physical "love" and the more inclusive "Love" notwithstanding, Pyrocles' "Love" encompasses physical desire. Granted the opportunity, Pyrocles, "fain . . . would have sealed with the chief arms of his desire, but Philoclea commanded the contrary; and yet they passed the promise of marriage" (I, 261). She feels the conflict between her love for Pyrocles on the one hand and her sense of honor on the other, a conflict that "made her fear to be alone with him, with whom alone she desired to be . . . " (I, 260). At last she cannot but give in to the external force of love, personified in the figure of her beloved, and say, "Thou hast then the victory: use it with virtue" (I, 260). Pyrocles shows the same sort of virtuous restraint in his turn and in him " . . . Love proved himself valiant, that durst with the sword of reverent duty gain-stand the force of so many enraged desires" (I, 261-62). Without undercutting the importance of sexuality in Love, then, the sequence beginning with Pyrocles' interview with Gynecia and Basilius on Gynecia's bed and ending with Pyrocles' revelation of his identity to Philoclea manages to suggest the difference between love and lust, commenting positively on the behavior of Pyrocles and Philoclea and negatively on that of Gynecia and Basilius.

The sequence also prepares for Pyrocles' narrative. Clearly the modulation from the main plot to Pyrocles' restrospective narrative is effected by Philoclea's request:

> what since [the end of the war with Tiridates] was the course of your doings, until you came, after so many victories, to make a conquest of poor me, that I know not, the fame thereof having rather showed it by pieces; than delivered any full form of it. Therefore, dear Pyrocles (for what can mine ears be so sweetly fed with as to hear you of you) be liberal unto me of those things which have made you indeed precious to the world, and now doubt not to tell of your perils; for since I have you here out of them, even the remembrance of them is pleasant. (I, 261)

Two facets of this request are immediately obvious. The injunction, "doubt not to tell of your perils," differentiates at the outset Pyrocles' narrative to follow from the earlier narrative of Musidorus, which had dealt with victories of "no more danger than glory" (I, 261). And Philoclea's remark, "since I have you here out of them [the perils], even the remembrance of them is pleasant," sums up the comic principle of *a priori* release of tension. This principle, of course, at least in part determines the effect of the retrospective narrations and surely explains why, for example, the audience discovers that Pamela loves Musidorus long before the prince discovers it. Philoclea must feel, moreover, that a talking Pyrocles is a good defense against an overly amorous Pyrocles.

Delasanta suggests that this modulation from main plot to delegated narration is less convincing than the preparation for Musidorus's narrative. He softens his criticism, however, by noting further that " . . . its very haste seems more appropriate to the precipitous characters of Pyrocles and [Philoclea] than a more deliberate, cautious narration like Musidorus's would have been."[39] But even thus attenuated, Delasanta's criticism neglects the rhetorical function of Pyrocles' narrative prepared for in this sequence. Lindheim points out that the rhetorical situations faced by the two princes during their retrospective narratives are fundamentally different. Whereas Musidorus has to show Pamela his nobility, Pyrocles has to demonstrate his integrity and ethical judgment. These are on shaky ground because of his disguise.[40] Lindheim's assertion is supported by Philoclea's ambivalence after Pyrocles' revelation, an ambivalence that results as much from the disguise as from the recognition of the sensual component of love.

> "Alas, how painful a thing it is to a divided mind to make a well-joined answer [to your confession and protestation of love]! How hard it is to bring inward shame to outward confession! and what handsomeness trow you can be observed in that speech, which is made one knows not to whom? Shall I say 'O Zelmane'? Alas your words be against it. Shall I say 'Prince Pyrocles'? Wretch that I am, your show is manifest against it. But this, this I may well say; if I had continued as I ought, Philoclea, you had either never been, or ever been Zelmane: you had either never attempted this change, set on with hope, or never discovered it, stopped with despair." (I, 260)

The unusually awkward and choppy syntax reflects the disturbance that Pyrocles' revelation has created in Philoclea's mind, a disturbance that concludes with the plea: "Thou hast then the victory: use it with virtue. Thy virtue won me; with virtue preserve me. Dost thou love me? Keep me then still worthy to be beloved" (I, 260-61). There is an ambiguity in Philoclea's use of the word "virtue": the "virtue" that won her appears to be Pyrocles' outward qualities, manifested through his disguise; the "virtue" that is to preserve her is the inner qualities that she hopes, rather than knows, he has. Pyrocles must demonstrate in his narrative that he has both kinds of "virtue." Thus this sequence establishes the rhetorical need for Pyrocles' narrative.

vii

The narrative delegated to Pyrocles is the densest part of the *Arcadia*. Whereas Musidorus's narrative is relatively straightforward with relatively discrete episodes, Pyrocles' narrative is marked by an interwoven plot and moral complexity. "The 'more complexly interwoven' style employed in Pyrocles' tales corresponds to the more difficult and exasperating lesson of his account, to the refusal of righted wrongs to remain settled."[41] The complexity of the account demonstrates rhetorically Pyrocles' integrity and ethical judgment, as Pyrocles makes clear when commenting on Andromana.

> Which proceeding of hers I do the more largely set before you (most dear lady) because by the foil thereof, you may see the nobleness of my desire to you, and the warrantableness of your favor to me. (I, 279)

In addition, the interweaving of the plot serves to show how an event, when placed in temporal perspective, is the product of a complex matrix of causes and is itself the cause of a complicated series of events. Abstractly and diagrammatically, an event placed in the context of both its causes and effects looks like a set of rays extending above and below the event:

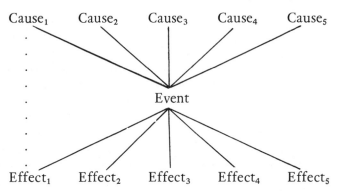

And because each cause and each effect is itself an event with its own context of causes and effects and because, for example, "$Effect_1$" might be directly tied to "$Cause_1$" (the dotted line) as well as indirectly through "Event," the temporal context expands in an irregular geometric progression. Pyrocles' narrative makes clear the complicated relationships between events. Thus, as his narrative proceeds, the causal chains become increasingly complex.

Because, however, Pyrocles' narrative is a narrative of events rather than the events themselves — the audience is continually reminded by Pyrocles' interjections to Philoclea that he is telling a· story — the episodes within the account are thematically as well as causally related. Each episode comments on the episodes preceding and following and on events in the main plot. For this reason, the easiest way to begin an approach to Pyrocles' narrative is to examine it as if the episodes were discrete. Such an examination should make the ethical complexity clear and expedite the causal analysis. For this purpose Pyrocles' narrative may be divided into three sequences: Pyrocles' encounters with Anaxius, Dido and ⁻Pamphilus, and Chremes; the episode at the Iberian Court, ending with. the suicide of Andromana; and the princes' adventures in Bythinia, the end of the story of Pamphilus, the rescue of Plexirtus, the combat in Pontus, ending with the second shipwreck.[42]

The stories of Anaxius's challenge to Pyrocles and of Pyrocles' involvement with Dido and the false Pamphilus, intertwined as they are, clearly parallel one another. Anaxius shows an excess of chivalric valor, which becomes pride; Pamphilus is governed by love reduced to its erotic component. The choices that Pyrocles must make are especially tenuous; he is forced to choose each time between evils and pick the lesser of the two. The sequence begins with a challenge from Anaxius and to show his moral worth to himself, which can now be shown to Philoclea by means of the narrative, Pyrocles decides to answer the challenge without the aid of Musidorus. But as he rides to meet Anaxius he encounters a curious sight: a man tied to the bottom of a tree surrounded by nine women who stab him with their bodkins and "sported themselves in his pain . . . " (I, 265). After he has driven away the ladies' knights and all but one of the ladies, the remaining lady, Dido, tells him " . . . because I see you are young, and like enough to have the power (if you would have the mind) to do much more mischief than he, I am content upon this bad subject to read a lecture to your virtue" (I, 265-66).

Pamphilus, it seems, has the bad habit of seducing and forsaking young women. He has been successful at this, each of the victims endeavoring to recover his affection, until "at length he concluded all his wrongs with betrothing himself to one (I must confess) worthy to be liked . . . " (I, 267). At this point, his ex-mistresses all banded together, vowed vengeance, and contrived to catch him alone in the forest. When confronted by his cast-off mistresses, Pamphilus justified himself with the sophistical argument that constancy in love consists of changing love objects for the sake of continued and varied pleasure. He then proceeded to point out the faults in each of his former mistresses, ending with Dido of whom he " . . . could find no other fault to object, but that (perdy) he met with many fairer" (I, 268). The catalogue of faults, says Dido, so incensed the ladies that they "laid hold of him; beginning at first but that trifling revenge, in which you found us busy; but meaning afterwards to have

mangled him so as [he] should have lost his credit for ever
abusing more" (I, 269).[43] While the punishment fits the
crime, it is rather brutal and Dido's motives include injured
pride as well as justice — "Many fairer? . . . I know (whoso-
ever says the contrary) there are not many fairer" (I, 269).
But then, friends of Pamphilus arriving, Pyrocles becomes
obligated to "forsake the ensign; under which I had before
served, and to spend my uttermost force in the protecting of
the lady . . . " (I, 269). He is, fortunately, able to establish an
uneasy peace, "And so I leaving her in a place of security (as
she thought) went on my journey towards Anaxius . . . "
(I, 269).

This is paradigmatic of the kinds of problems that con-
front Pyrocles throughout the rest of his narrative. Both of
the parties in the Dido-Pamphilus confrontation are, to a
greater or lesser degree, in the wrong. There is nothing admirable in Pamphilus's practice of seeking sexual satisfaction·
at the expense of nine women; his sophistical justification of
the practice shows his fundamental viciousness as does his
cry to his friends "that they should kill that woman, that had
thus betrayed and disgraced him" (I, 269). His behavior, if it
typified the erotic drive, would justify Miso's remarks on the
nature of love. But the crude and brutal justice proposed by
Dido and the other ladies is likewise inhuman and untenable.
The fact that Pyrocles is forced to change sides in his intervention suggests that changes in situation change the nature
of ethical choice. The uneasy peace at the end of the confrontation, moreover, vindicates no one other than Pyrocles
and settles nothing beyond the immediate moment. It will
come as no surprise, then, that the Dido-Pamphilus conflict
erupts again shortly afterwards. The moral choice that Pyrocles has had to make has been particularly difficult and the
action consequent upon that choice, inconclusive.

With the Pamphilus-Dido matter apparently settled, Pyrocles goes forth to meet Anaxius. Arriving at the place desig-
nated by Anaxius, Pyrocles awaits his opponent because
Anaxius insisted that Pyrocles "stay two days in the appointed

place, he disdaining to wait for me, till he was sure I were there" (I, 269). Anaxius's arrival and the beginning of the duel are simultaneous: "And as soon as ever he can near me, in fit distance for his purpose, he with much fury (but with fury skillfully guided) ran upon me . . . " (I, 270). Anaxius's behavior in matters of chivalry parallels Pamphilus's in matters of love; each refuses to abide by the rules governing these spheres of human action. Anaxius is driven by pride and anger while Pamphilus is driven by pride and desire.

After nondecisive exchanges on horseback, the duel continues on foot,[44] until interrupted by the flight of Dido and pursuit of Pamphilus. Although Pyrocles requests permission to leave the fight to aid "this distressed lady" (I, 271), promising to return another day, Anaxius refuses and Pyrocles is forced to make another moral decision. Either he must risk his reputation as a knight by refusing to continue the duel or he must neglect his duties as a knight by ignoring a lady in distress. The dilemma is real; as Pyrocles goes in Dido's aid, the "country folks, who happened to pass thereby, . . . hallooed and hooted after me as at the arrantest coward, that ever showed his shoulders to his enemy" (I, 271). In making the choice he does, Pyrocles chooses the fact of knighthood over the name of knighthood. It is therefore possible to make moral choices even in complex situations, but the choices are not without their cost. But this accords with the rhetorical function of Pyrocles' narrative — to demonstrate his ethical judgment to Philoclea.

After a six-hour chase, Pyrocles finally catches up with Dido, Pamphilus, and Pamphilus's troop in time to prevent the multiple rape and murder of Dido in front of her father's "old ill-favored castle" (I, 272). Dido's father, the miserly Chremes, grudgingly lets Dido and Pyrocles stay the night, but once he discovers Pyrocles' identity he plots an ambush against his guest in order to turn the prince over to Artaxia for the reward she has offered.[45] Although this threat is thwarted by the fortuitous arrival of the King of Iberia, it shows that virtuous action does not necessarily produce extrinsic rewards. This has the effect of compounding ethical issues by separating the problem of rewards and punishments from the decision-making process. Pyrocles made the ethically right choice in choosing to leave the fight with Anaxius and follow Dido and Pamphilus, but that choice leads to the threat of punishment rather than to a reward. Moreover, the death of Dido indicates that ethical choice is no guarantee of the efficacy of moral action. The ambiguity of decision made explicit in the Dido-Pamphilus episode forces our recognition of the difficulties of ethical choice and moral action in a fallen world. This is less true of the other episodes of the *Arcadia*, so the Dido-Pamphilus episode has a unique tone.[4][6]

The second portion of Pyrocles' narrative divides neatly into two parts: the first deals with the princes' imprisonment at the hands of Andromana and the second with their escape with the aid of Palladius and Zelmane. After being rescued from Chremes' ambush by the King of Iberia, Pyrocles and Musidorus, who rejoined his friend during the ambush, go with their rescuer to his kingdom. There they meet the wanton Andromana who has, for all intents and purposes, taken over ruling the kingdom of Iberia so that " . . . all his subjects having by some years learned so to hope for good, and fear of harm, only from her, that it should have needed a stronger virtue than his, to have unwound so deeply an entered vice" (I, 278). Andromana's penchant for lustful behavior, already manifested in her adulterous liaison with Plangus, asserts itself again with the two princes. "For, with equal ardor she affected us both: and so did her greatness disdain shamefastness, that she was content to acknowledge it to both" (I, 278). Because the princes resist her illicit attentions she has them imprisoned, using as her excuse to the King that " . . . we went about some practice to overthrow him in his own estate" (I, 280). Her explanation is accepted "because of the strange successes we had had in the kingdoms of Phrygia, Pontus and Galatia . . . " (I, 280). The princes' virtuous victories come back to haunt them and serve as a cause of punishment rather than reward. Andromana's behavior clearly parallels Pamphilus's earlier in that she too has had so many affairs that " ... it seemed, for a last delight, that she delighted in infamy ... " (I, 278-79). Pamphilus's vice is therefore not, strictly speaking, a specifically masculine fault. And in Pamphilus and Andromana the audience is given extreme examples of the vice that afflicts Basilius and Gynecia in the main plot.

Pyrocles juxtaposes the stories of Andromana and Pamphilus with the story of Palladius's love for Zelmane and Zelmane's for himself.[47] Thus he reinforces the double attitude toward love implicit throughout the *Arcadia*. The two princes must choose between being "restrained to so unworthy a bondage" (I, 280), which is clearly wrong, and responding to Andromana's overtures, "that to grant, had been wickedly injurious to him, that had saved our lives: and to accuse a lady that loved us, of her love unto us, we esteemed almost as dishonorable ... " (I, 280). Pyrocles' summarizing remark on this situation and on the way they are to get out of it clarifies the complexity of love:

> But while we were thus full of weariness of what was past, and doubt of what was to follow, Love (that I think in the course of my life hath a sport sometimes to poison me with roses, sometimes to heal me with wormwood) brought forth a remedy unto us: which though it helped me out of that distress, alas the conclusion was such, as I must ever while I live, think it worse than a rack, so to have been preserved. (I, 281)

The oxymora "poison me with roses" and "heal me with wormwood" suggest the failure of an absolutist position on love. They also suggest that while the behavior of Pamphilus and Andromana ought not to be the sole basis for an analysis of love and its effects, their behavior must be accounted for in such an analysis. As Pyrocles looks ahead — "alas the conclusion was such" — he reminds the audience that the consequences of ethical choice are ambiguous and so continues that thread so firmly established in the Dido-Pamphilus episode.

The second half of this section of Pyrocles' narrative, anticipated in his remark cited above, properly begins with "Iber-

ian yearely justes" instituted by the King as a celebration of
his and Andromana's anniversary. This tourney clearly parallels Phalantus's tourney in Book I; both arise out of a man's
false love for a wicked woman, and the courses of the two are
parallel. Things go badly for the side on which Pyrocles and
Musidorus are to fight until they enter the action. And just as
there was the comic challenge of the shepherd, Lalus, in
Phalantus's tourney, there is the comic match between the
shepherd, Philisides, and Lelius in the Iberian tourney.[48] The
parallels between the two tourneys, however, emphasize the
significant difference between them: in Phalantus's tourney
the princes fought on the "right" side but in the Iberian
jousts their situation forces them to fight on the "wrong"
side, against Helen and her knights. This accords with the
ethical ambiguity that permeates Pyrocles' narrative.

In addition to reinforcing the ethical complexity of Pyrocles' narrative, the Iberian jousts provide the *raison d'être* for
the description of Helen of Corinth who, succeeding her
father to the throne, " . . . using so strange, and yet so well-
succeeding a temper, . . . made her people by peace, warlike;
her courtiers by sports, learned; her ladies by love, chaste"
(I, 283). Helen's rule of Corinth, then, contrasts markedly
with the rule of Andromana in Iberia, just as the two women
are virtually opposite types. The parallels between this description and Musidorus's description of Euarchus earlier
clearly show that the virtues necessary for wise and just rule
are not strictly masculine virtues, just as the vices of Plexirtus and Pamphilus are not specifically masculine vices.[49]
Finally, Pyrocles uses Helen to demonstrate to Philoclea
that love does not necessarily lead to a disintegration of
virtue: although she is committed to loving Amphialus, Pyrocles argues, " . . . yet is neither her wisdom doubted of, nor
honor blemished" (I, 284). Then, in a vein that has immediate application to his and Philoclea's situation, he argues
that love, wisdom, honor, and greatness of heart must necessarily be tied together.

The Iberian jousts enable Pyrocles and Musidorus to escape

from Andromana. Zelmane's love for Pyrocles causes her to persuade Palladius to help the princes out of prison. Unable to convince the King, his father, that he should release them, he decides to use guile and, since the tourney is going badly for the Iberian host, persuades his mother to allow the princes to participate. He then leads them past the armed guard that Andromana had placed just to prevent their escape. The threesome flee into Bithynia, where they are overtaken by Andromana; in the ensuing battle Palladius is killed in spite of Andromana's command "to take us alive, and not to regard her son's threatening therein . . . " (I, 287).[50] The death of Palladius is a direct consequence of Andromana's lust, for it comes at the hands of one of her former lovers, who mistakes Palladius for one of the princes and kills him out of jealousy. This clearly suggests that viciousness can destroy innocence and that disaster may not result from guilt but simply from situation. Palladius's death, then, reminds us that the reward for moral action is not extrinsic, or at least not necessarily so. The suicide of Andromana that follows, and is the consequence of, the death of her son ends the princes' adventures in Iberia and the second portion of Pyrocles' narrative.

The final portion of Pyrocles' exposition begins with the conclusion of the story of Pamphilus.[51] Pyrocles and Musidorus, "having recommended those royal bodies . . . to be conveyed to the King of Iberia" (I, 288), encounter "a fair gentlewoman, whose gesture accused her of much sorrow, and every way showed she cared not what pain she put her body to, since the better part (her mind) was laid under so much agony . . . " (I, 289). This is Leucippe, to whom Pamphilus had been betrothed and whom he had forsaken in favor of Baccha, "the most impudently unchaste woman of all Asia . . . " (I, 290). The princes take Leucippe to a nunnery, "where she resolved to spend all her years (which her youth promised should be many) in bewailing the wrong, and yet praying for the wrongdoer" (I, 290). Leucippe's complaint, however, forces Pyrocles to make another ethical decision.

He is tempted, because of Pamphilus's involvement in the death of Dido, to seek out the philanderer and exact revenge upon him. The situation makes the decision easy and Pyrocles chooses to leave him to Baccha because " . . . it should be a gain to him to lose his life, being so matched . . . " (I, 290). The wisdom of this decision has been attested to by Andromana's behavior, she being the same sort of wanton as Baccha, and by the fact that revenge as a motive is suspect in the *Arcadia*. Each of the characters who is driven by revenge is also shown to be morally flawed. Anaxius is a prime example of this. Even Amphialus, although essentially noble, is flawed in his desire for revenge on Helen for her part in the death of Philoxenus. The consequences of this flaw become fully revealed in the civil war that occupies Book III. Thus this incident provides Pyrocles with another example of his moral judgment to show Philoclea.

The morning after they leave Leucippe in the nunnery, Pyrocles and Musidorus are joined by Zelmane who, because of her love for Pyrocles, has disguised herself as the page Daiphantus. The three of them then settle a civil war in Bythinia. As an adventure, the Bythinian affair resembles the adventures described at much greater length in Musidorus's narrative. Thus Pyrocles' brevity clearly confirms the fundamental distinction between his and Musidorus's narratives; Musidorus needs to show his nobility and Pyrocles to show his integrity.

Having settled the civil war, the princes start home. But even before they have left the confines of Bithynia, they "beheld one of the cruellest fights between two knights, that ever hath adorned the most martial story" (I, 292). The "two knights" are Tydeus and Telenor, who have been set at each other's throats by the treachery of Plexirtus. From these two unfortunates Pyrocles and Musidorus learn of Plexirtus's behavior after Leonatus's ascension to the throne of Paphlagonia (Galatia), of his attempt to poison Leonatus, his mission to Trebisonde, and his successful plot against Tydeus and Telenor. The reappearance of Plexirtus in the retrospective narratives fulfills the anticipation left at the end of Musidorus's narrative and reminds the audience of the inconclusive nature of moral action. After berating themselves for the folly of having misspent their lives in the faithful service of one "who did not love faithfulness," Tydeus and Telenor warn the princes not to place their "good will upon any other ground, than proof of virtue . . . ," because no man can be "good to other, that is not good in himself" (I, 294-95). They recognize their share of responsibility in their downfall, confirming the sense of human responsibility that permeates the story of the "*Paphlagonian* unkind King" and reminding the audience of the importance of human weakness in the efficacy of evil in the world.

This bears on the death of Zelmane, caused by her mourning her father's treachery and her fear for him when she learns of the threat to him posed by the old Paphlagonian knight. Although her death results in large part from her father's behavior, it also results from her unrequited love for Pyrocles. But if her love of Pyrocles is somewhat in error, the error is not what she thinks, is not that she is unworthy.

> Such was therein my ill destiny, that this young lady Zelmane (like some unwisely liberal, that more delight to give presents, than pay debts) she chose (alas for the pity) rather to bestow her love (so much undeserved, as not desired) upon me, than to recompense him, whose love (besides many other things) might seem (even in the court of honor) justly to claim it of her. (I, 282)[5 2]

While the fault is minimal — Pyrocles, after all, is surely a lovable young man — it allowed her father's evil to destroy her and to almost destroy Pyrocles and Musidorus. Nevertheless, as she dies she asks Pyrocles to aid Plexirtus, who has been trapped by the revengeful old Paphlagonian knight. Pyrocles does so, and once again that villain survives to plague the two princes with his machinations.

While Pyrocles is saving Plexirtus, Musidorus is busy defending the King of Pontus from the onslaught of "Otanes

(brother to Barzanes, slain by Musidorus, in the battle of the
six princes [in the Erona-episode] " (I, 296). After Pyrocles
rejoins his successful friend, they are celebrated by

> great multitudes of many great persons, and even of princes; especially
> those, whom we had made beholding unto us: as, the Kings of
> Phrygia, Bithynia, with those two hurt [in the fight with Otanes
> and the two giants], of Pontus and Galatia [Paphlagonia], and
> Otanes the prisoner, by Musidorus set free; and thither came Plexir-
> tus of Trebisonde, and Antiphilus, then King of Lycia;[53] with as
> many mo great princes, drawn either by our reputation, or by
> willingness to acknowledge themselves obliged unto us, for what we
> had done for the others. (I, 301-2)

This catalogue brings together the important personages in
each of the retrospective narratives related thus far in Book II
and so anticipates the close of Pyrocles' tale. The adventures
in Asia are at an end and the princes decide to travel to Arcadia. In part their decision is the result of the information
that " . . . Anaxius with open mouth of defamation had gone
thither to seek me" (I, 302) and is spreading malicious stories
of Pyrocles through the courts there. Thus the princes are
again moved forward because of past events; again the significance of an event is changed by a change in temporal
perspective.

Plexirtus's pretended repentance fools Pyrocles and Musidorus and his treachery mars their trip to Arcadia. They travel
in a ship provided by that villain and Plexirtus has commanded
its captain to murder the princes. An old counselor, fortunately
won over by the princes' virtue, reveals the plot to Pyrocles
and Musidorus and promises to aid them. When the captain
calls for the sailors to strike the princes down, the old counselor opposes him. What follows is

> a most confused fight. For the narrowness of the place, the darkness
> of the time, and the uncertainty in such a tumult how to know
> friends from foes, made the rage of swords rather guide, than be

guided by their masters. For my cousin and me, truly I think we never performed less in any place, doing no other hurt, than the defense of ourselves, and succoring them who came for it, drove us to: for not discerning perfectly, who were for, or against us, we thought it less evil to spare a foe, than spoil a friend. But from the highest to the lowest part of the ship there was no place left, without cries of murdering, and murdered persons. The captain I happed awhile to fight withal, but was driven to part with him, by hearing the cry of the counsellor, who received a mortal wound, mistaken of one of his own side. (I, 305)

Lindheim rightly calls this a "fit culmination to the cousins' stay in Asia Minor"; it is "not an example of practice moralized to fit the framework of an educational theory, but an instance of the ambiguous, unclassifiable world itself."[54] It fitly sums up the ethical complexity that has been building throughout the retrospective narratives, beginning as far back as Musidorus's tale of the Paphlagonian King. Because the episode is an extreme example of moral complexity, it warns the audience away from applying moral absolutes even to the apparently much simpler main plot.

The numerous allusions in the final portion of Pyrocles' narrative to significant aspects of the main plot anticipate the almost immediate return to the main plot of the *Arcadia*. Zelmane's dying request that Pyrocles and Musidorus adopt the names Daiphantus and Palladius upon their arrival in Greece is the most obvious of these and explains the otherwise inexplicable aliases taken by the princes upon their arrival in Laconia. Moreover the disguise chosen by Zelmane in order to be with Pyrocles psychologically justifies his choice of the Amazonian disguise to get access to Philoclea. His choice of the name "Zelmane" clearly satisfies Zelmane's wish that he "have cause to remember me." Finally, Zelmane's appearance prefigures Philoclea's, and her sacrifice thus predisposed Pyrocles to love Philoclea.

For I must confess for true, that if my stars had not wholly reserved me for you, there else perhaps I might have loved, and (which had been most strange) begun my love after death: whereof let it be the less marvel, because somewhat she did resemble you: though as far short of your perfection, as herself dying was of herself flourishing: yet something there was, which (when I saw a picture of yours) brought again her figure into my remembrance, and made my heart as apt to receive the wound, as the power of your beauty with unresistable force to pierce. (I, 299)

Thus the final portion of Pyrocles' narrative anticipates the return to the main plot and clarifies issues that earlier were more or less obscure.

The episodes in Pyrocles' narrative are not, however, discrete but causally interrelated, both among themselves and with the other retrospective narratives of Book II. The interrelationships create much of the ethical ambiguity and complexity of events and choices in Pyrocles' narrative; they show temporal perspective to be an important factor in both ethical judgment and causal analysis. Thus each event related by Pyrocles has a myriad of causes and effects on even the most immediate levels. The war between Tiridates and Erona, first reported in Philoclea's story of Erona, serves as an example of this. Included among the direct causes of this conflict are Plangus's problems with his father and step-mother, Tiridates' desire to marry Erona, her love for Antiphilus, and the aid offered Erona by Pyrocles and Musidorus. The conclusion of the war includes among its effects: Artaxia's ascension to the throne of Armenia, Erona's marriage to Antiphilus, Anaxius's challenge of Pyrocles, and the assault on Pontus by Otanes and the two giants. Thus, the diagram of the war between Tiridates and Erona, placed in its context of causes and effects — in its temporal context, as it were — would look like this:

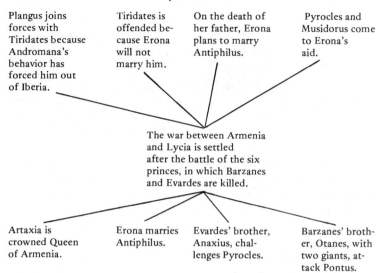

From this it is obvious that every event is the apex of two pyramids built in opposite directions and that, once placed in wide temporal context. apparently discrete events prove to be causally related. This is manifested in two ways in Pyrocles narrative. On the one hand, events have effects far beyond the immediate context. The battle of the six princes, for example, directly causes Anaxius's challenge; and after the duel between Anaxius and Pyrocles is interrupted, the proud knight defames Pyrocles in Peloponnesus, prompting the princes to go to Arcadia. Thus their decision to travel to Arcadia has its roots in the conflict between Tiridates and Erona. On the other hand, conflicts apparently settled by the virtuous action of the two princes continually reassert themselves and thus become related to events with which otherwise they would have no connection. In the story of Pamphilus, for example, the interruption of the duel between Anaxius and Pyrocles by Pamphilus's pursuit of Dido not only is part of the causal chain leading from the battle between

Tiridates and Erona to the princes' departure for Arcadia, but
also involves the princes in the domestic crises in Iberia. Thus
Pyrocles' narrative suggests the importance of causal sequences, of the interrelationship of events in time. As far as his
narrative is characteristic of Book II, it suggests an emphasis
on temporal process.

Finally, like the stories of Erona and Plangus earlier, Pyrocles' narrative involves both the erotic and the political themes
in the temporal emphasis of Book II — perhaps because the
ethical judgment that Pyrocles is demonstrating to Philoclea
bears on both realms. Thus, for example, Andromana's erotic
behavior has the effect of determining the political situation
of Iberia. Not only does she become the *de facto* ruler of
Iberia after her marriage to Plangus's father but she has her
son, Palladius, named heir apparent because Plangus refuses
to renew his liaison with her after her marriage. And in Dido's
remark, "And a man may see, even in this, how soon rulers
grow proud, and in their pride foolish . . . " (I, 268), the
political theme is drawn into a story that is fundamentally
erotic. Although Musidorus's narrative emphasizes the political over the erotic and Pyrocles' emphasizes the erotic over
the political, the two are clearly not fully separate modes of
behavior but are rather, perhaps, the same behavior under
different perspectives. It follows, moreover, that schematizing
the differences between the narratives of Pyrocles and Musidorus is likely to obscure the carefully stressed and essential
relationship between political and erotic behavior.

viii

When Pyrocles has finished his narrative, he persuades
Philoclea to complete the story of Erona, but they are interrupted by Miso, who then reports back to Gynecia that Philoclea and "Zelmane" have been alone. This puts Gynecia
squarely on the horns of a dilemma. Basilius sees no reason
why the two young people should be kept separated and his
wife is unwilling to reveal Pyrocles' sex, for she knows that

would mean at least his immediate expulsion from the pastoral retreat. "Fain she would have barred her daughter's hap, but loath she was to cut off her own hope" (I, 309). Gynecia's problem parallels the ethical decisions made by the princes in the retrospective narratives. But it is different in two important ways. Clearly Gynecia must choose between two unethical actions: barring "her daughter's hap" and cutting "off her own hope" of an adulterous affair with Pyrocles. And her dilemma, unlike those faced by the princes, has strong comic overtones. The audience is aware both of Pyrocles' virtuous antipathy to adultery, manifested earlier in his refusal of Andromana, and of the lovers' vows exchanged by Pyrocles and Philoclea; thus we find it difficult to take Gynecia's problem seriously.

Comedy is also present in Gynecia's love complaint, which follows and which parallels Philoclea's earlier love complaint (I, 173-74). In this instance, however, the comedy reinforces the serious message of the complaint, for both are directed against Gynecia's illicit love.

> "O jealousy," said she, "the frenzy of wise folks, the well-wishing spite, and unkind carefulness, the self-punishment for others' fault, and self-misery in others' happiness, the cousin of envy, daughter of love, and mother of hate, how could'st thou so quietly get thee a seat in the unquiet heart of Gynecia, Gynecia," said she sighing, "thought wise, and once virtuous? Alas it is thy breeder's power which plants thee there: it is the flaming agony of affection, that works the chilling access of thy fever, in such sort, that nature gives place; the growing of my daughter seems the decay of myself; the blessings of a mother turn to the curses of a competitor; and the fair face of Philoclea, appears more horrible in my sight, than the image of death. (I, 309-10)

That Gynecia is in a position to make this complaint is surely comic, but the ethic implicit in the complaint is not. Her jealousy results from her love which, because adulterous, inverts normal matronly pleasures into pains by disrupting the family structure. Moreover, because the resulting agony must be held inward, it destroys the self as well:

These fires increase: in these I daily burn:
They feed on me, and with my wings do fly:
My lovely joys to doleful ashes turn:
Their flames mount up, my powers prostrate lie:
They live in force, I quite consumed die.

                                                        (I, 310)

So, beset by these emotions, Gynecia goes to break up the *tête-à-tête* of the lovers and, after sending Philoclea home, makes further advances to Pyrocles.

These overtures are, however, interrupted by the intrusion of the Arcadian rebels. And just as Gynecia's illicit love represents an overthrow of the family structure and an inversion of motherly values, the Arcadian rebellion is an attempt to overthrow the political structure and carries with it an inversion of civilized values. This last is most clear in the rebels' attack on Gynecia and "Zelmane." By ignoring the sex of their intended victims the rebels violate established social norms and convert females from centers of life to focuses for death. In so doing they replace order with chaos. It is therefore fitting that their attack lack order and the attackers be "all knit together only in madness" (I, 311). The loss of order corresponds to the chaotic scene aboard ship during the second shipwreck and thus expands the imagery of chaos from the private sphere of Plexirtus's plot against the princes to the public arena of the body politic of Arcadia.

Although the rebellion poses a potentially serious threat, the rebels are treated here with black humor. The death of the tailor should serve as an example:

> Yet among the rebels there was a dapper fellow, a tailor by occupation, who fetching his courage only from their going back [the retreat of Basilius and company], began to bow his knees, and very fencerlike to draw near to Zelmane. But as he came within her distance, turning his sword very nicely about his crown, Basilius, with a side blow, struck off his nose. He (being a suitor to a seamster's daughter, and therefore not a little grieved for such a disgrace) stooped down, because he had heard, that if it were fresh put to, it would cleave on again. But as his hand was on the ground to bring his nose to his head, Zelmane with a blow, sent his head to his nose. (I, 312)

The dark comedy, however, is directed exclusively against the rebels. It serves, therefore, as additional criticism of their behavior and, incidentally, of the concept of democracy as well. When Pyrocles, putting words in Basilius's mouth, commands the rebels to "set down, and choose among yourselves someone, who may relate your griefs or demands unto him" (I, 315), they are unable to come to any agreement among themselves; each social group speaks only for itself and at the expense of all the others. They finally turn to what amounts to internecine squabbling. Sidney uses this episode, then, to justify monarchy as a political system and to indicate the difficulties of a democratic system of government.[55]

Of perhaps greater importance, however, is the cause of the uprising. Behind it lies the mysterious figure of Cecropia, whose bear and lion disturbed the pastoralism at the end of Book I and whose agent, Clinias, instigated this rebellion by inflaming the people with a whispering campaign against Basilius and his viceregent, Philanax. The Arcadian rebellion thus parallels the episode of the lion and bear in that both anticipate the greater role played by Cecropia's ambition in Book III. Yet the responsibility for the uprising is not Cecropia's alone; Basilius is responsible as well. One lesson of the retrospective narratives is that the individual is at least partially responsible for what happens to him. Clinias explains how the rebellion grew out of the celebration of Basilius's birthday and points out the role played by Basilius's retreat in the people's discontent.

> But being once well chafed with wine (having spent all the night, and some piece of the morning in such revelling) and emboldened by your absented manner of living, there was no matter their ears had ever head of that grew not to be a subject of their winey conference. (I, 322)

The "winey conference" produced the idea "that it was time to come and see; and if you were here, to know (if Arcadia were grown loathsome in your sight) why you did not rid yourself of the trouble?" (I, 323).

But as mischief is of such nature, that it cannot stand but with strengthening one evil by another, and so multiply in itself, till it come to the highest, and then fall with his own weight: so to their minds (once passed the bounds of obedience) more and more wickedness opened itself, so that they who first pretended to preserve you, then to reform you (I speak it in my conscience, and with a bleeding heart) now thought no safety for them, without murdering you. (I, 324)

This mob psychology clearly shows that, although Cecropia has helped matters along, the rebellion results directly from Basilius's abdication of royal responsibility.

The Arcadian rebellion, settled by Pyrocles' use of language, leads to the revelation of the cause of Basilius's retreat from royal responsibility and the recitation of the oracle alluded to in Philanax's letter in Book I.

> Thy elder shall from thy careful face
> By princely mean be stolen, and yet not lost.
> Thy younger shall with Nature's bliss embrace
> An uncouth love, which Nature hateth most.
> Both they themselves unto such two shall wed,
> Who at thy bier, as at a bar, shall plead;
> Why thee (a living man) they had made dead.
> In thy own seat a foreign state shall sit.
> And ere that all these blows thy head do hit,
> Thou, with thy wife, adultery shall comit.

(I, 327)

The first four lines of this oracle are, in spite of Basilius's willful misinterpretation of them, clear to the audience: the "princely mean" by which Pamela shall be stolen is Musidorus and the "uncouth love, which Nature hateth most" is the disguised Pyrocles. Since the first part of the oracle[56] is accurate, the last five lines create audience anticipation of the *Arcadia*'s ending. This anticipation is reinforced by Gynecia's earlier prophetic dream, which supplements the Delphic oracle:

It seemed unto her to be in a place full of thorns, which so molested her, as she could neither abide standing still, nor tread safely going forward. In this case she thought Zelmane, being upon a fair hill, de-

lightful to the eye, and easy in appearance, called her thither: whither
with much anguish being come, Zelmane was vanished, and she found
nothing but a dead body like unto her husband, which seeming at
the first with a strange smell to infect her, as she was ready likewise
within awhile to die; the dead body she thought took her in his arms,
and said, "Gynecia, leave all; for here is thy only rest." (I, 308)

The appearance in Book II of Gynecia's dream, like the delay-
ing of the prophecy, [57] has the effect of stressing the book's
temporal emphasis; like the oracle, the dream transcends time
for its effect.

ix

With the Arcadian rebellion as settled as was the situation
in Paphlagonia at the end of Musidorus's narrative, and the
reason for Basilius's retreat revealed, Pyrocles asks Basilius
to relate the remainder of the Erona-Plangus story. Basilius
accedes, and the story he tells reflects ironically on his own
behavior and it ties together some of the temporal strands
remaining loose at the close of the other retrospective narratives.

After the princes leave Erona and Antiphilus settled in the
Kingdom of Lycia, Antiphilus shows his baseness. He displays
neither training nor inclination for ruling wisely, and he takes
the crown for license and presumes "that what he did was
liked of everybody: nay, that his disgraces were favors, and
all because he was a king" (I, 330). Basilius's retreat, though
not so obviously misrule as Antiphilus's licentiousness, shows
the same sort of lack of political wisdom. A king ought to
recognize merit in his subjects and to show by his presence
similar and consistent virtue; in Philanax's words: "Let your
subjects have you in their eyes; let them see the benefits of
your justice daily more and more; and so must they needs
rather like of present sureties, than uncertain changes" (I, 25).
Basilius, moreover, relies on the oracles in much the same way
as Antiphilus relies on flatterers.

> Whereto nothing helped him [Antiphilus] better, than that poison-
> ous sugar of flattery: which some used, out of the innate baseness of
> their heart, straight like dogs fawning upon the greatest; others se-
> cretly hating him, and disdaining his great rising so suddenly, so un-
> deservedly (finding his humor) bent their exalting him only to his
> overthrow; like the bird that carries the shellfish high, to break him
> the easier with his fall. (I, 330)

Against this description of flatterers can be set Philanax's advice to Basilius:

> wisdom and virtue be the only destinies appointed to man to follow,
> whence we ought to seek all our knowledge, since they be such
> guides as cannot fail;[58] which, besides their inward comfort,[59] do
> lead so direct a way of proceeding, as either prosperity must ensue;
> or, if the wickedness of the world should oppress it, it can never be
> said, that evil happeneth to him, who falls accompanied with virtue.
> . . . These kinds of sooth-sayings [oracles] (since they have left us
> in ourselves sufficient guides)[60] to be nothing but fancy, wherein
> there must either be vanity, or infallibleness, and so, either not to be
> respected, or not to be prevented. (I, 24)

Finally, Antiphilus's misbehavior is another argument against
democracy: those not born to rule are unfit to rule, "For in
nature not able to conceive the bounds of great matters (suddenly borne into an unknown ocean of absolute power) he
was swayed withal (he knew not how) as every wind of
passions puffed him" (I, 330).

Antiphilus subverts the legal structure by passing "an un-
lawful law of having mo wives than one" (I, 331), and courts
Artaxia with the hopes of becoming the King of Armenia.
Because she holds a grudge against Erona and Antiphilus for
their part in the death of Tiridates, and hopes to trap them,
Artaxia consents to the polygamous marriage. Imprisoned
and threatened with death, Antiphilus quickly breaks down
while Erona, "sad indeed, yet like one rather used, than new
fallen to sadness (as who had the joys of her heart already
broken) seemed rather to welcome than to shun that end of
misery . . . " (I, 332). Her bearing causes Plangus to fall in

love with her. She persuades him to help the wretched Antiphilus out of prison. His failure to engineer Antiphilus's escape shows that the similar though successful efforts by Palladius on behalf of Pyrocles and Musidorus depended on their virtues as well as on the unfortunate loves of Palladius and Zelmane. Although Plangus cannot prevent the execution of Antiphilus, he is able to delay Erona's. Aided by "some principal noblemen of that country" (I, 355), he captures Artaxia's bastard nephew and threatens him with the same fate as Erona. Forced to come to terms with Plangus, Artaxia then stays the execution until the second anniversary of Tiridates' death and places Erona for sake-keeping until that date in the castle of a neutral noble. If in the interim Pyrocles and Musidorus were to come and defeat two knights appointed by Artaxia, she agrees to free Erona; otherwise, the hapless queen is to be burned. Plangus, therefore, leaves to seek out the princes in Greece, but on the way he intercepts letters written by Artaxia convincing him that the princes are dead and informing him that Artaxia and her new husband, Plexirtus, have violated the truce. Basilius's continuation of the Plangus-Erona story ends with Plangus's decision to seek out Euarchus's aid.

In addition to providing parallels to events in both the main plot and the retrospective narratives, this continuation ties together the loose threads of the other retrospective narratives. In addition to eliminating Antiphilus from the ongoing cast of characters, it links the Plexirtus line with the Artaxia line so that, just as the principal good recipients of Pyrocles and Musidorus's aid were gathered together at the end of Pyrocles' narrative, the major surviving villains are here gathered together. It can be said, therefore, that Basilius's share of the Plangus-Erona story is a second apex of the temporal pyramids built up by the retrospective narratives.

x

Basilius's narrative is a fit conclusion to a book that deals through its structure with the workings of temporal process. It is also fitting that a book whose most important events occur in retrospective narratives should end with a retrospective narrative. A balance between reason and passion as two important components of human behavior has been struck, and it is with this balance that the Second Eclogues begin.

Just as the First Eclogues began with a dance performed by lovers, requited and unrequited, at the end of which all the dancers joined together to sing of the necessity of love, the Second Eclogues begin with "a dance, which they called the skirmish betwixt Reason and Passion" (I, 339). The poetic dance opens upon the apparent disjunction between reason and passion:

> REASON. Can Reason then a tyrant counted be?
> PASSION. If Reason will, that Passions be not free.
> R.   But Reason will, that Reason govern most.
> P.   And Passion will, that Passion rule the roost.
>
> (I, 339)

Yet reason and passion are not held in disjunction throughout either the *Arcadia* or this song; the latter concludes:

> . . . the two square battles meet, and instead of fighting embrace one another, singing thus:
> R.   We are too strong: but Reason seeks no blood.[61]
> P.   Who be too weak, do fain they be too good.
> R.   Though we cannot o'ercome, our cause is just.
> P.   Let us o'ercome, and let us be unjust.
> R.   Yet Passions yield at length to Reason's stroke.
> P.   What shall we win by taking Reason's yoke?
> R.   The joys you have shall be made permanent.
> P.   But so we shall with grief learn to repent.
> R.   Repent indeed, but that shall be your bliss.
> P.   How know we that, since present joys we miss?
> R.   You know it not: of Reason therefore know it.
> P.   No Reason yet had ever skill to show it.
> R. P.   Then let us both to heavenly rules give place,
>   Which Passions kill, and Reason do deface.
>
> (I, 340)

Just as the dance that began the First Eclogues suggested the ultimate harmony of the lovers meeting in Basilius's retreat, this dance suggests the harmony that is the result of the proper balance of reason and the passions. And this balance applies equally well to both the political and the erotic spheres of human behavior.

The second two poems in the Second Eclogues deal specifically with the erotic motif. The first of these is a dialogue in which Dicus quizzes Musidorus on the progress of his love. Davis sees this poem as a debate between the passionate Dorus and the reasonable shepherd Dicus.[62] Davis, however, neglects Dicus's reason for engaging Musidorus in the dialogue:

> Dicus (that had in this time taken a great liking of Dorus, for the good parts he found above his age in him) had a delight to taste the fruits of his wit, though in a subject which he himself most of all other despised: and so entered to speech with him in the manner of this following eclogue. (I, 340)

It also neglects Dicus's wish that "thou soon may have some help, or change of passion" (I, 343), that either the prince's love prove more accessible or he have a change of heart. Instead of being an anti-love poem, in fact, the dialogue is a good-natured though not very serious "flyting" on the nature of love, in which the manner of expression counts more than its content. Moreover, the ensuing comic version between Nico and Pas reduces the chances of its being taken seriously. The poems' light-hearted treatment of the erotic contrasts with the seriousness of the tone of the retrospective narratives and, like the comic interruptions by the main plot of the retrospective narratives, rhetorically releases tension.

The final two poems of the eclogues, "I joy in grief" and "Fair rocks, goodly rivers, sweet woods," return to the serious mood of the retrospective narratives and so anticipate the serious events that are to begin the third book of the *Arcadia*. These eclogues, then, balance the comic and the serious in much the same way that the comic and the serious have been balanced throughout the book, and their emphasis on the erotic motif balances the emphasis on the political theme in the retrospective narratives.

Notes

1. Wolff, p. 353.

2. Lawry notes that Sidney "causes tales of the princes' adventures in Asia Minor to master time, as they simultaneously make a lasting general instruction for the princes . . . " (p. 198). Lawry's discussion emphasizes the latter point while this discussion will emphasize the former.

3. One of the best discussions of the problems of the presentation of time that I know of is Hans Meyerhoff, *Time in Literature* (Berkeley, Calif., 1955).

4. Ricardo J. Quinones, *The Renaissance Discovery of Time, Harvard Studies in Comparative Literature* 31 Cambridge, Mass., 1972): 27. Quinones argues persuasively that the problem of time was of central concern to the Renaissance. His argument suggests, moreover, that Nancy Rothwax Lindheim's discussion of the distinction between episode and fable [*ELR* (1972)], however useful it is in identifying thematic centers, may finally be too restrictive. If the argument concerning temporal perspective presented here is correct, then it is likely that the events in the retrospective narratives (episodes) would have been resolved in the main plot (fable) in a completed version of the *Arcadia*. On this, of course, the oracle is silent.

5. David C. McPherson's suggestion that a possible source for Mopsa is the engraving *The Wedding of Mopsus and Nisa* published at Antwerp in 1570 from a drawing by Pieter Bruegel the Elder visually augments the sense of comedy implicit in Musidorus's mock courtship of Mopsa ("A Possible Origin for Mopsa in Sidney's *Arcadia*," *Renaissance Quarterly* 21 [1968]: 420-28).

6. The royal birthmark used by Musidorus for identification is a fairly frequent device in the romance form and is found, for example, in Tasso's *Rinaldo*, Boiardo's *Orlando Innamorato*, and Spenser's *Faerie Queene* (cf. Edmund Spenser, *The Works: A Variorum Edition*, ed. Edwin Greenlaw, et al., 9 vols. [Baltimore, 1932-1949], 6: 260-64, 371-81; citations from Spenser in my text are to this edition). In most instances, however, the birthmark identifies a foundling or stolen child; here it is Musidorus's means to circumvent his disguise.

7. Rodney Delasanta, speaking of the difference between Musidorus's narrative and Pyrocles' narrative later in Book II, argues that " . . . Musidorus uses the occasion of the narrative to reveal his identity to Pamela, his narrative thus becoming a kind of prelude to their love . . . " (p. 74). Insofar as he is speaking of the summary biography, there can be no question about this. But the major portion of Musidorus's narrative occurs after Pamela's discovery of his identity

and her admission to her sister, and hence to the audience, that she loves him as well. In this sense Delasanta's remark is misleading.

8. The term *discrepant awareness* is taken over from Bertrand Evans, *Shakespeare's Comedies* (New York, 1960). The appearance of Sebastian in *Twelfth Night* (I, ii) serves, according to Evans's discussion, a function similar to that served by the revelation that Pamela returns Musidorus's love (pp. 121-24).

9. The problem of the narrator and the audience's role in the *Arcadia* is discussed somewhat more fully in the preceding chapter.

10. Incidentally, the negative values of the words applied to love by the narrator in this section ought to be taken as a function of the internalization of the audience rather than as indicative of the narrator's value system. Thus the rhetorical effect of such language is to make felt the force of love rather than giving an evaluation of that force. The alternative reading, to see the language as primarily evaluative, establishes a contradiction between the language of the *Arcadia* and its narrative sequence, which asserts love as a potential good.

11. William and Melleville Haller, "The Puritan Art of Love," *HLQ* 5 (1942): 235-72 and William Haller, " 'Hail Wedded Love,' " *ELH* 13 (1946): 79-97. Mark Rose's *Heroic Love* deals extensively with the problem of chastity and love in Sidney and Spenser. He claims that the Elizabethans approved of passionate love only insofar as it led to married love. But this, as Rose notes, became paradoxical: "Marriage was now a supreme goal, but to reach this goal one first had to yield to passionate love – and this, from the point of view of humanist ethics, was still morally suspect" (p. 34). Rose's point is especially applicable to the sense of love that the *Arcadia* imparts.

12. Haller's description of these two books briefly demonstrates this concept of chastity as it is found in Spenser: "When Spenser in *The Faerie Queene* comes to the virtues he names chastity and friendship, his poem resolves itself in a fabric of interlacing tales of unmatched, mismatched friends and lovers, sorting themselves into pairs, seeking each his or her own proper mate and spiritual counterpart. The base souls, though they may begin in seeming amity, conclude in strife and hatred. The nobler spirits, no matter how they begin, all end in love and peace and, with one exception [Balphoebe], in the bonds of matrimony" (" 'Hail Wedded Love,' " p. 89).

13. Although it would be overly ingenious to carry the analogy between Erik Erikson's psychological theory and the events in the *Arcadia* very far, his remarks on "falling in love" during the "fifth age of man" (identity *versus* role confusion) seems appropriate to Philoclea's situation: "This initiates the stage of 'falling in love,' which is by no means entirely, or even primarily, a sexual matter – except where the mores demand it. To a considerable extent adolescent love is an attempt to arrive at a definition of one's identity by projecting one's diffused ego image on another and by seeing it thus reflected and gradually clarified. This is why so much of young love is conversation" (*Childhood and Society*, 2d ed. [New York, 1963], p. 262).

14. "Sidney's *Arcadia* as Elizabethan Allegory," p. 332.

15. Myrick, p. 296. The issue of teaching in the *Arcadia* is Myrick's topic for the whole of his chapter "Poetic Truth in the *New Arcadia*," pp. 229-97, but he is careful, more careful than Greenlaw, not to attempt to make the *Arcadia* over into a treatise.

16. Tillyard, p. 307.

17. The term *primary auditor* is arbitrarily chosen to distinguish an audience that is wholly internal — that is, an audience made up of a character or characters of the *Arcadia* — from the audience which, although its characteristic responses are defined by the work, is external to it — that is, readers of the *Arcadia*. The term *primary auditor* is not meant to imply more than that disjunction.

18. *A Map of Arcadia*, p. 121.

19. Besides, Nancy Rothwax Lindheim is surely right when she claims that Davis's argument shares the fault of oversimplification with Greenlaw's argument ("Sidney's *Arcadia*, Book II: Retrospective Narrative," *SP* 64 [1967] : 161).

20. Delasanta, pp. 74-75. Delasanta's conception of Musidorus's character follows that laid down by John Danby in opposition to Pyrocles' character (*Elizabethan and Jacobean Poets*, pp. 56-58).

21. "Retrospective Narrative," pp. 162-63.

22. It should be noted in passing that Musidorus here confirms Philanax's advice to Basilius concerning oracular knowledge (I, 24) when he comments on Phrygia's attempt to change the predicted future: "Foolish man, either vainly fearing what was not to be feared, or not considering, that if it were a work of the superior powers, the heavens at length are never children" (I, 188).

23. Musidorus and Pyrocles are separated before they land after escaping from the shipwreck, just as they are to be separated again following the second shipwreck (the one with which the *Arcadia* begins). In this instance Pyrocles arrives safely on the shores of Phyrgia and Musidorus on the shores of Pontus.

24. "Retrospective Narrative," p. 170.

25. There is a slight inconsistency here, the only one noted by Wolff (p. 353 n33). Although the country is here named "Galatia,"and will so be called everywhere else ("Galatia" alternates with "Galacia") save once, Leonatus refers to it as "this country of Paphlagonia" (I, 208). Wolff's explanation of scribal error seems likely. Besides, who would recognize the story of the "Galatian unkind King"?

26. The sense of modernity implicit here is liable to be deceptive. It must be remembered that the late Greek romances frequently involved more complex

structures of choice than the medieval English romance. And there is similar narrative convolution in Books III and IV of the *Faerie Queene* and in Ariosto's *Orlando Furioso*. In fact, similarity in plot structure between Sidney's work and Ariosto's leads Freda Townsend to conjecture that Sidney owed a debt to the Italian in that regard (pp. 97-108).

27. Most studies that deal with this section of the *Arcadia*, however, are concerned primarily with the relationship between Shakespeare's plays and Sidney's work and as a consequence are less than rigorous in their treatment of Sidney. Included in such studies are: Fitzroy Pyle, " 'Twelfth Night,' 'King Lear' and 'Arcadia,' " *MLR* 43 (1948): 449-55; D. M. McKeithan, "*King Lear* and Sidney's *Arcadia*," University of Texas, *Studies in English* 14 (1934): 45-49 (which deals more with the story of Plangus than with that of the Paphlagonian King); and Irving Ribner, "Sidney's *Arcadia* and the Structure of *King Lear*," *Studia Neophilologica* 24 (1952): 63-68. Of these studies, only Ribner's deals in any detail with the relationship between the story of the Paphlagonian King and the main plot of the *Arcadia*. Although it is suggestive to see the former narrative as a comment on Basilius's behavior as Ribner does, Ribner seriously distorts Sidney's work when he sees it as dealing in essence solely with politics.

28. This example of the soft-hearted thieves is a frequent device in traditional romances and is reminiscent of Valentine's encounter with the outlaws in *Two Gentlemen of Verona*. It is often, as it is here at least implicitly, a demonstration of the way Providence protects the virtuous from the unjust assaults of parental figures prompted by evil forces, and as such is a comic motif.

29. There is a curious difference between the plays of Shakespeare that deal in a fundamental way with what may be called political theory, notably *Richard II*, and these episodes in Sidney's *Arcadia*. In both the Phrygia and the Pontus episodes, the tyrant who is deposed is the legitimate ruler of his country but the question of legitimacy does not arise, only the question of the adequacy of the king's rule. It follows, then, that the doctrine implicit in these episodes is concerned only with the nature of right ruling and, by extension, the problem of "the bad king" does not arise under this theory. In *Richard II*, however, right rule (Bolingbroke) is set againsg legitimate rule (Richard), so that the problem of "the bad king" is a fundamental issue of the play. It does not follow from this that Sidney was a less rigorous thinker in such matters than was Shakespeare, merely that the problem to be solved was different for the two. Sidney was concerned with ideal politics, while Shakespeare seems to have been interested in practical politics.

30. As Lindheim puts it, "It is not the princes themselves who have changed in Pyrocles' account of their exploits, but the kind of situations with which they must deal. And this change in turn limits the effectiveness, while increasing the moral difficulty, of their actions" (p. 169).

31. The Freudian terms *wish* and *defense* are borrowed from Norman Holland's *The Dynamics of Literary Response* (Oxford, 1968), for which definitions see his glossary.

32. Delasanta, p. 70.

33. *A Map of Arcadia*, pp. 121-22.

34. Chaucer, of course, was following Boccaccio's example, for Troilo commits the same offense and is similarly punished; Mirabella, in the *Faerie Queene*, also offends Cupid by rejecting her many suitors and for this must do penance "Which was, that through this worlds wyde wildernes/She wander should in companie of those,/Till she had sau'd so many loues, as she did lose" (*The Faerie Queene*, VI. vii.37). For references to this motif in folklore, see Stith Thompson, *Motif-Index of Folk-Literature*, rev. and enlarged ed., 6 vols. (Bloomington, Ind., 1956), 5: 186 (Q 4), 202-7 (Q 220), and particularly 241 (Q 499.7).

35. Danby, pp. 57-60 *passim*. It would, of course, be unwise to push this distinction very far. Nevertheless, two modern critics, Lawry and Dennis, have picked up and extended Danby's interest in sexual polarity. Lawry sees, for example, Musidorus's retrospective narrative as dealing with "the masculine world of heroism" and the other retrospective narratives as dealing with the feminine world of passion (pp. 209-40). Dennis, on the other hand, divides the princes and princesses according to their kinships with nature or civilization: Pyrocles is the man of nature; Philoclea, the woman of nature; Musidorus is the man of civilization; Pamela, the woman of civilization (pp. ix-xiv). Such polarities are informative but if rendered too baldly distort the *Arcadia*, since Sidney is careful to indicate that the vices and virtues he reveals are not restricted to one or the other sex. Pamphilus and Andromana, for example, are marred by essentially the same vice and Euarchus and Helen are marked by the same sorts of virtues.

36. Oddly enough, Ringler misses this particular bit of comedy, for in his commentary on the poem he takes the identification with Cupid at face value and remarks "that the hundred-eyed Argus begot Cupid on Io is Sidney's invention" (*Poems*, p. 387).

37. *A Map of Arcadia*, p. 123.

38. *Ibid*., p. 122.

39. Delasanta, p. 67.

40. Lindheim, p. 163.

41. *Ibid*., p. 180. Much of Lindheim's analysis rests on this distinction between the narrative of Musidorus and that of Pyrocles.

42. The division is similar to one suggested by Lindheim (p. 174) and differs only in the division of parts two and three. The segmentation suggested here accords with the chapter divisions of the *Arcadia* and the third part proves to be a gathering of the various threads handled in this and the earlier retrospective narratives of Book II.

43. In his article, "The Dido Incident in Sidney's 'Arcadia,' " *N&Q*, n.s. 3, 201 (1956), D. M. Anderson suggests that the punishment in store for Pamphilus can be read as emasculation (p. 418).

44. Anaxius is forced to the ground by the accidental death of his horse. "He driven to dismount, threatened, if I did not the like, to do as much for my horse, as fortune had done for his. But whether for that, or because I would not be beholding to Fortune for any part of the victory, I descended" (I, 270-71). Anaxius's behavior upon the death of his horse is clearly a product of his attributing to Pyrocles the sort of attitudes that he himself holds. And, Pyrocles' disclaimer notwithstanding, Anaxius's attitudes contrast with those of his opponent.

45. This episode has a marked resemblance to the Malbecco episode in *The Faerie Queene* (III, ix-x) and Malbecco and Chremes clearly belong to the same literary family as does the figure of Jealousy in Gascoigne's *The Adventures of Master F. J.*, which may provide the source for both Sidney and Spenser.

46. It is the uniqueness of this episode that leads D. M. Anderson to conjecture that it has its source in the Italian *novella* (pp. 418-19).

47. Pyrocles' motivation for including mention of the loves of Palladius and Zelmane at this point is obviously to prevent the instillation of anti-love attitudes in Philoclea, his primary auditor. The inclusion works, of course, the same effect on the audience of the *Arcadia*.

48. Philisides is, as has often been noted, a partial anagram for Philip Sidney. Moreover, the situation of Philisides for "one (they say) that was the Star, whereby his course was only directed" (I, 285) may be an amalgamation of *Astrophil and Stella* sonnets 41 and 53 (*Poems*, pp. 185, 191).

49. Pyrocles' description of Helen shows Philoclea his ability to recognize right rule just as Musidorus's description of Euarchus showed Pamela his ability to recognize a good ruler. These two descriptions, then, parallel each other in rhetorical function.

50. There is a parallel between Andromana's apparent willingness to sacrifice her son to satisfy her lust and Chremes' earlier willingness to sacrifice his daughter because of his greed. This parallel suggests the essential similarity between kinds of viciousness and is reinforced by the similarity between the deaths of the two characters.

51. This is the last mention of Pamphilus in the revision as far as it goes. It is, however, quite likely that he would have appeared once again toward the end of the *Arcadia* had the revision been completed.

52. This is, of course, also a comment on Amphialus's love of Philoclea, which has already been revealed and which is to have such disastrous consequences in the next book, when he is loved by the virtuous and worthy Helen.

53. It is worth noting that the two evil characters included in this catalogue are set apart from the others by the syntax, just as they are set apart by their evil natures.

54. Lindheim, p. 168.

55. Alan D. Isler comments extensively on this scene and notes that "Sidney's first concern is to condemn riot; decorum dictated that he treat the encounter between nobles and rabble-in-arms comically. But he certainly makes no effort to flesh out his individual rioters in such a way as to engage our sympathies in their behalf" ("Sidney, Shakespeare, and the "Slain-Notslain,' " *UTO* 37 [1967-1968]: 184). Isler is surely correct in claiming that the cartoonlike characteristics of the rabble preclude an accusation of cruelty against Sidney for the way in which the princes dispose of them.

56. The accuracy of the oracle in no way abrogates Basilius's folly in acting upon it, especially to avoid the future it predicts. This has been made clear by Phrygia's abortive attempts to circumvent the predictions made at Musidorus's birth.

57. In the *Old Arcadia* the prophecy is related early in Book I.

58. The wisdom of the remark is confirmed in another context by the advice passed on to Pyrocles and Musidorus by Tydeus and Telenor after their unfortunate duel.

59. Of course it is the "inward comfort" of "wisdom and virtue" that is of the greatest importance, for the retrospective narratives make it clear that the only necessary reward for virtue is intrinsic rather than extrinsic.

60. The implication of this is that oracular wisdom is fallible since it must be interpreted by humans, and the consequence of that is clearly demonstrated by Basilius's willful misinterpretation of the oracle.

61. Pulling this line out of its immediate context suggests the underlying antipathy of the *Arcadia* toward the revenge motive; revenge is unreasonable.

62. *A Map of Arcadia*, p. 100.

4

Book III and the Structure of Value

i

The first two books of the *Arcadia* do not indicate the way in which values are structured. In the erotic sphere, love operates both as a positive force, as with Argalus and Parthenia, and as a negative force, as with Dido and Pamphilus. Although positive love may be called "love," and negative love "lust," this distinction has necessarily been based on the different consequences of the two motives and it sometimes presents difficulties. While Zelmane's love for Pyrocles, for example, clearly differs in kind from Andromana's lust for the two princes, it also differs from Parthenia's for Argalus, and these differences correspond to the ambivalent consequences of Zelmane's love for Pyrocles. Similarly, the loves of Helen, Amphialus, and Plangus are, at least in terms of their consequences, difficult to categorize as either love or lust; those either/or categories are probably inadequate to explain those characters' motives. Finally, Erona's infatuation with Antiphilus is surely faulty in much the same way as Phalantus's love for Artesia was faulty. But whereas Phalantus's behavior skirts disaster, Erona's has catastrophic consequences.

The same sort of difficulty arises with the political theme. The good ruler Euarchus and the tyrannical old Kings of Phrygia and Pontus stand at opposite ends of the political spectrum. But here, as in the erotic sphere, evaluative labels are not adequate to cover the range of political behavior included in the *Arcadia*. Plangus's father, the King of Iberia, is neither a simple tyrant nor a good ruler. Though the old King of Paphlagonia's weakness contributed to his downfall, he was, nonetheless, a better ruler than his bastard son, Plexirtus. Basilius's retreat into the forest of Arcadia may be a political error, but it does not make him the bad ruler that Antiphilus proves to be.

The difficulties with the either/or categories arise partly from the ethical complexity built up through the temporal emphasis of Book II. As the causal chains became more and more intertwined, the princes' choices became more and more ambiguous. In breaking off the duel with Anaxius and following Dido and Pamphilus, Pyrocles chose the lesser of two evils, losing honor by leaving the duel rather than by refusing to help a lady in distress. Although the audience clearly ought to agree with Pyrocles' decision, their approval comes not from an established value system but partly from intuition and partly from their trust in Pyrocles. But this implies that either ethical decisions must be made intuitively, a notoriously unreliable way, or made by an exemplary man. This subverts the didactic component of the *Arcadia* and suggests that it is solely oriented toward the pleasure motives of the audience.

Though the *Arcadia* is neither a treatise nor an explication of a particular, historically established value system, Ficino's or anyone else's, we cannot deny the didactic component of the work. Sidney's own critical and theoretical bias includes the concept of *dulce et utile* rather than pleasure without utility. For him, literature is "a speaking *Picture*, with this end to teach and delight" (III, 9). The two ends of poetry go hand in hand in Sidney's theory of poetry, for poets "imitate both to delight and teach, and delight to move men to take that goodnesse in hand, which without delight they would flie as from a stranger; and teach to make them know that goodnesse wherunto they are moved . . . " (III, 10). Sidney's expressing the concept of *dulce et utile* in his *Apology for Poetry* does not neccessarily mean that he applied that theory to the *Arcadia*. But that work accords completely with the principle of *dulce et utile*. Having dealt, in the first two books, with the spatial and temporal ways in which the world is structured, the *Arcadia* goes on to create a structure of value[1] and to test one value system against another. Thus the emphasis in the third book is neither spatial nor temporal, but normative. It does not, however, lose its sense of narrative and become a treatise.[2]

While the normative emphasis of Book III is most evident in the interspersed debates, of which the one between Pamela and Cecropia on atheism is the best known, the issue itself is first raised in the transitional first chapter, which begins with a change in Pamela:

> This last day's danger [the fight with the Arcadian rioters], having made Pamela's love discern, what a loss it should have suffered, if Dorus had been destroyed, bred such tenderness of kindness in her toward him: that she could no longer keep love from looking out through her eyes . . . (I, 354)

Besides yoking the third book to the second, this opening sentence begins the emphasis on the problem of value. The slight shift in Pamela's behavior results from her reevaluation of Musidorus's worth, and the worth of love. She does not find the problem easy. When Musidorus, perceiving the change in her attitude, attempts to kiss her, she immediately puts him away from her. On the one hand, she has perceived a new worth in Musidorus; on the other, she is still unwilling to make the sort of commitment that her new values would seem to dictate. Her problem is a slighter version of Amphialus's problem later in the book. The speech with which she temporarily shunts Musidorus aside employes the language of norms and judgment:

> "Away," said she, "*unworthy* man to love, or to be loved. Assure thyself, I hate myself for being so *deceived; judge* then what I do thee, for *deceiving* me. Let me see thee no more, *the only fall of my judgment*, and *stain of my conscience*." (I, 355; italics mine)

Pamela's use of the intimate "thee" instead of the impersonal "you" takes some, but by no means all, of the sting out of her reaction to Musidorus's attempted theft of a kiss. Despite her rejection of him, she is ambivalent in her values, torn between her sense of his worth and her unwillingness to commit herself.

When Pamela rejects his kiss, Musidorus despairs of "being fallen from all happiness" (I, 355) and becomes introspective and self-contemptuous. Just as Amphialus, after the death of Philoxenus, fled into the woods in his despair, Musidorus "remained . . . two days in the woods, disdaining to give his body food, or his mind comfort, loving in himself nothing, but the love of her" (I, 356). But love persuades him to give up the attempt at suicide by starvation and "to seek some means by writing to show his sorrow and testify his repentance" (I, 356). The description of the epistle to Pamela he then writes and its being one of Sidney's experiments in quantitative verse both testify the labored quality of Musidorus's epistle. The sophistry that Pamela uses to persuade herself to read the epistle — "it were not much amiss to look it over, that she might out of his words pick some further quarrel against him" (I, 357) — is like Musidorus's arguments against starving himself, and suggests a conflict of values. This conflict is not, however, resolved by her reading the letter, an act not motivated by rational analysis but performed "e're she were aware." And although the rhetorical function of Musidorus's epistle is "to show his sorrow and testify his repentance," it too raises the question of norms without overtly positing a satisfactory solution.

> Shall I not? O may I not thus yet refresh the remembrance,
>> What sweet joys I had once, and what a place I did hold?
> Shall I not once object, that you, you granted a favor
>> Unto the man, whom now such miseries you award?
> Bend your thoughts to the dear sweet words which then to
>> me giv'n were:
>> Think what a world is now, think who hath alt'red her heart.
> What? Was I then worthy such good, now worthy such evil?
>> Now fled, then cherished? Then so nigh, now so remote?
>
> (I, 359)

Faced by the same problem as Astrophil in sonnet 86 (*Poems*, p. 212), Musidorus uses the same sort of approach: he implies the invalidity of Pamela's position but fails to demonstrate the values that make the position invalid. "What this would have wrought in her, she herself could not tell: for, before her reason could moderate the disputation between favor and faultiness" (I, 359), Pamela is interrupted by Philoclea and Miso. So the question of value, of normative systems, is raised, but not answered; this interchange establishes the issue that will be emphasized throughout Book III in both the political and the erotic themes.

ii

Without having resolved the question of value implicit in Musidorus's epistle, Pamela is joined by her sister, Miso, and Pyrocles. As they sit "devising how to give more feathers to the wings of time . . . " (I, 360), the young people are approached by "six maids, all in one livery of scarlet petticoats" (I, 360) who attempt to persuade them to join some pastoral festivities. But instead of the expected pastoral interlude, the princesses and Pyrocles are the victims of an ambush planned by Cecropia, who plotted to "have sent these goodly inheritrixes of Arcadia to have pleaded their cause before Pluto . . . " (I, 365). Her scheme to convert Pan, a figure of fecundity, to Pluto, the god of death, is changed only at the last moment because " . . . overfortunately for them, you [Amphialus] made me know the last day how vehemently this childish passion of love doth torment you" (I, 365).

Several points about the capture are immediately obvious. The princesses and Pyrocles attend the pastoral only because Miso insists. Up to this point, Basilius's error in appointing Dametas and his family guardians of Pamela has been merely a nuisance. But with the abduction of Pamela, Philoclea, and Pyrocles, the guardianship by the clowns takes on catastrophic implications. This indicates the fine line drawn in the *Arcadia* between the purely comic and the serious, between minor and major errors. The very nature of the trap, a pastoral exercise turned into a military ambush, shows the thorns lurking under the placid pastoral aspect of the *Arcadia*: here it corresponds to the attack of the lioness and bear in the first book. Finally, since Amphialus's love changes Cecropia's plans from the execution of her captives to their imprisonment, the erotic and political themes of the *Arcadia* are at once intertwined in the captivity episode; love ameliorates the political evil of Cecropia even though she knows that " . . . hate often begetteth victory; love commonly is the instrument of subjection" (I, 365).

The interrelationship of the two themes in the captivity episode is further established in Cecropia's explanation to Amphialus of what she had done and her reasons for so doing. Basilius had remained "unmarried till he was nigh threescore years old (and in all his speeches affirming, and in all his doings assuring, that he never would marry) . . . " (I, 363). So, with the expectation that he was Basilius's heir, Basilius's younger brother arranged a match with Cecropia, the daughter of the King of Argos. In this marriage, Cecropia's sole object was to speedily become the Queen of Arcadia, "for else you may be sure the King of Argos, nor his daughter would have suffered their royal blood to be stained with the base name of subjection" (I, 364). After the birth of Amphialus, her ambition prompted her even to hurry the occasion of her royal ascension by plotting against Basilius's life. But the plot is cut short by her husband's death, an event she attributes to the envy of the heavens. Cecropia's marriage, then, which ought to be erotically motivated, has a political basis. The political action of capturing the princesses and Pyrocles, on the other hand, is significantly modulated by the erotic motive of her son, Amphialus. Thus, the particular interrelationship of the two themes found here suggests a confusion of values, a confusion rooted primarily in Cecropia's egotism. "Did I go to church? It seemed the very gods waited for me, their devotions not being solemnized till I was ready" (I, 364). Besides being blasphemous, Cecropia's egotism is, in a sense, an attempt to impose her own values on the world, an attempt that cuts her off from those around her in much the same way as Anaxius's egotism isolates him.

Amphialus is not deeply involved with Cecropia's plots. The *Arcadia* explicitly denies that he has any part in her designs against Basilius and his family. The Arcadian uprising was "quite without the consent of Amphialus, who would not for all the kingdoms of the world so have adventured the life of Philoclea" (I, 319). His relative innocence resembles that of Tydeus and Telenor and is narratively required if he is to be "an excellent son of an evil mother" (I, 363). But his relative innocence in the actual plotting does not absolve him of all culpability, as he himself admits to Philoclea.

> "Dear lady," said he, "I will not say unto you (how justly soever I may do it) that I am neither author, nor accessory unto this your withholding. For since I do not redress it, I am as faulty as if I had begun it." (I, 369)

Amphialus's failure to act on this existential awareness of responsibility until much later, when he discovers the depths of

Cecropia's evil actions, indicates the infectious quality of her egotism.

Amphialus allows Philoclea's imprisonment to continue, even though he knows that it is wrong, because he is caught between his ethical sense and his love for Philoclea, and his mother plays on his conflicting emotions.[3] When, in response to Cecropia's partially true claim that she captured the princesses for his sake, he accuses his mother of hindering the progress of his love by displeasing Philoclea, she cynically agrees to release the captives. To this Amphialus objects, " . . . since she is here, I would not for my life constrain presence, but rather would I die than consent to absence" (I, 366). Cecropia rightly notes that Amphialus's arguments are "pretty intricate follies," for he has confused political expediency and egocentric love. Philoclea's reply to his first suit shows clearly the nature of Amphialus's confusion.

> "Alas cousin," said she, "what shall my tongue be able to do, which is informed by the ears one way, and by the eyes another? You call for pity, and use cruelty; you say, you love me, and yet do the effects of enmity. You affirm your death is in my hands, but you have brought me to so near a degree to death, as when you will, you may lay death upon me: so that while you say I am mistress of your life, I am not mistress of mine own. You entitle yourself my slave, but I am sure I am yours. If then violence, injury, terror, and depriving of that which is more dear than life itself, liberty, be fit orators for affection, you may expect that I will be easily persuaded."
> (I, 368)

In short, in keeping Philoclea prisoner Amphialus inverts the situation so frequently described in Elizabethan love poetry in which the lover is conquered by the beloved or by Cupid, who has taken up residence in her.[4] One succinct example of this device, found in *Astrophil and Stella*, should help to make Amphialus's confusion of values clearer:

> Faire eyes, sweet lips, deare heart, that foolish I
> Could hope by *Cupid's* helpe on you to pray;

Since to himselfe he doth your gifts apply,
As his maine force, choise sport, and easefull stay.
    For when he will see who dare him gainesay,
Then with those eyes he lookes, lo by and by
Each soule doth at *Love's* feet his weapons lay,
Glad if for her he give them leave to die.

(*Poems*, p. 186)

The attitude here expressed is in marked contrast to the attitude implicit in Amphialus's behavior in the *Arcadia*; and this contrast is at the core of Philoclea's reply to his suit.

Besides confusing his erotic values in the dialogue with Philoclea, Amphialus confuses political values in his justification of the abduction of the two princesses. Acknowledging "how much the duty which is owed to the country, goes beyond all other duties . . . " (I, 371), he argues "that since the end whereto anything is directed, is ever to be of more noble reckoning, than the thing thereto directed: that therefore, the weal-public was more to be regarded, than any person or magistrate that thereunto was ordained" (I, 371-72). Granted the nature of his duty, Amphialus claims that his present concern for Arcadia results from Basilius's retreat, from his placing the reins of government in the hands of Philanax — "a man neither in birth comparable to many, nor for his corrupt, proud, and partial dealing, liked of any" (I, 372) — and from his endangering Pamela and Philoclea by depriving them of proper protection.[5] His justification rests upon a combination of "some glosses of probability, [which] might hide indeed the foulness of his treason" (I, 371), and is rhetorically designed "from true commonplaces, [to] fetch down most false applications" (I, 371). Amphialus is partially right in speaking of the duty owed to one's country and he carefully avoids being charged with rebellion against a duly anointed lord; ostensibly he is acting in the king's best interests. "And if the prince should command them [the subjects of Arcadia] otherwise, yet to know, that therein he was no more to be obeyed, than if he should call for poison to hurt himself withal . . . " (I, 372). Amphialus is also partially right in mentioning the risk to the princesses that results from Basilius's retreat. The fact that Cecropia is able to have them kidnapped is ample evidence. But the justification is only half true; it depends on the false premise that Philanax is "a man neither in birth comparable to many, nor for his corrupt, proud, and partial dealing, liked of any . . . . " Amphialus justifies himself, then, only by turning certain commonplaces of Elizabethan political doctrine to his own use and by urging the populace to support politically an action that is in actuality erotic and egocentric.

The justification, however it may distort Elizabethan political doctrine and reflect Amphialus's confusion of values, is but part of his defense against the expected military action of Basilius. And in this regard Amphialus's "rhetorical colors" are an effective part of the defense " . . . which as they prevailed with some of more quick than sound conceit, to run his fortune with him; so in many did it breed a coolness, to deal violently against him, and a false-minded neutrality to expect the issue" (I, 373).[6] Judging from the apparent success of the justification, confusion of values need not impede efficiency of action, at least in such terms as the values will allow. This judgment is further corroborated by Amphialus's skill in preparing the defense of the castle, particularly the defense army. The shrewdness of his battle plans contrasts with the chaos attending the Arcadian uprising in Book II, chaos directly resulting from the fact that "everyone commanded, none obeyed, he only seemed chief captain, that was most rageful" (I, 311). Amphialus seeks not many commanders, "contenting himself, that the multitude should have obeying wits . . ." (I, 373). His military ability causes Basilius's siege of the castle to be totally unsuccessful, at least until Amphialus finally recognizes the fullness of his mother's evil and changes his position late in Book III. Between Cecropia and Amphialus, then, there is a strong suggestion that, although values ought not to be structured egotistically, a confusion of values does not necessarily bar effective action, at least in certain realms.

iii

Although Amphialus's confusion of values does not prevent him from intelligently establishing the defenses of the castle, the very fact that he must do so shows that confusion of values leads to untenable positions. Thus he is able to commit himself to either Cecropia's assertive values or the integrative values of love — he can neither rape Philoclea nor set her free — and he allows Cecropia's egotism free reign. She, in turn, plans to court Philoclea for Amphialus, "not doubting the easy conquest of an unexpert virgin, who [*i.e.,* Cecropia] had already with subtlety and impudency begun to undermine a monarchy" (I, 376). Cecropia "doubted not at least to make Philoclea receive the poison distilled in sweet liquor, which she with little disguising had drunk up thirstily" (I, 376). Clearly, then, the wicked queen plans to seduce Philoclea with exactly those values which Cecropia herself embraces; she plans, therefore, to impose her values on the princess.

Cecropia begins the seduction with a *carpe diem* argument.

"Look upon your own body, and see whether it deserve to pine away with sorrow: see whether you will have these hands" (with that she took one of her hands and kissing it, looked upon it as if she were enamored with it) "fade from their whiteness, which makes one desire to touch them; and their softness, which rebounds again a desire to look on them, and become dry, lean and yellow, and make everybody wonder at the change, and say, that sure you had used some art before, which now you had left? For if the beauties had been natural, they would never so soon have been blemished." (I, 376-77)

This argument, although not fully developed here, suggests that the foci of Cecropia's erotic values are beauty and pleasure. But, as Raleigh points out in "The Nymph's Reply to the Shepherd," the *carpe diem* argument contains its own counterargument: if beauty and pleasure are transient, then they are inadequate foundations of value.

> The flowers do fade, and wanton fields
> To wayward Winter reckoning yields;
> A honey tongue, a heart of gall,
> Is fancy's spring, but sorrow's fall.

When beauty fades — seasons change; winter must come — a value structure based on the ideal of beauty crumbles. *Carpe diem*, which depends on seasonal change for its rhetorical force, assumes a structure of values that is logically valid only if the seasons do not change and winter — old age — does not come. Raleigh's nymph shows her awareness of this:

> But could youth last, and love still breed,
> Had joys no date, nor age no need,
> Then these delights my mind might move
> To live with thee and be thy love.

Philoclea's refusal to respond to Cecropia's opening gambit implies that she, like Raleigh's nymph, realizes the invalidity of the *carpe diem* argument's denial of natural process. This inference is made the easier by the negative and rather unattractive form in which Cecropia couches her argument with its emphasis on the "dry, lean and yellow" consequences of age and its concern for what others might think of Philoclea when Philoclea herself has clearly ignored the possibility of using art to affect those who have imprisoned her.

Philoclea's being "an unexpert virgin," which made Cecropia think her an "easy conquest," turns out to be an effective defense and explains Philoclea's reticence in replying to the spurious arguments. Philoclea's natural innocence protects her, for example, when Cecropia tries to excite female curiosity. "But she [Philoclea], who rather wished to unknow what she knew, than to burden her heart with more hopeless knowledge, only desired her to have pity of her, and . . . to grant her liberty . . . " (I, 377). The fact that Philoclea does not fall into the trap, besides showing the protective quality of her natural innocence, suggests the inadequacy of projecting attributes and of predicting other people's behavior from the way one acts oneself.

Because her ruse to trap Philoclea with "female inquisitiveness" has failed and because of Philoclea's single-minded desire for liberty for herself and her companions, Cecropia shifts the grounds of her attack. She now argues that, since marriage to Amphialus is the only means to liberty, Philoclea should marry Amphialus and so be free. She asks Philoclea if she would turn away "some heavenly spirit" (I, 377) offering liberty merely because the spirit wanted to go through a back door rather than through the main entrance: "Would you not drink the wine you thirst for, without it were in such a glass, as you especially fancied?" (I, 378). Cecropia's obvious presupposition, that the goal justifies the means, implies that the liberty purchased through marriage to Amphialus is liable to be costly, an implication confirmed by Cecropia's later plans to court both princesses for her son, "using the same arguments to the one sister, as to the other; determining that whom she could win first, the other should (without her son's knowledge) by poison be made away" (I, 401). Cecropia's egotism, manifested in the metaphor of the "heavenly spirit" for her son,[7] allows no scruples to stand in the wicked queen's way. The figure of the wine, moreover, carries with it particularly malevolent undertones from Cecropia's earlier image of "the poison distilled in sweet liquor" (I, 376) and the poison that she plans to use on the princess who fails to accept Amphialus. Fortunately, just as the earlier attempt to trap Philoclea through curiosity failed, this more egotistical argument to get the princess to marry Amphialus also fails.

Cecropia then argues against virginity and for marriage; and these arguments, like the *carpe diem* argument, emphasize her equating love and sexuality. Her reply to Philoclea's claim that she has vowed "to lead a virgin's life to my death . . . " (I, 379),[8] although overtly based on the very life processes that the *carpe diem* argument implicitly denied, climaxes with the pleasures of sexual intercourse: Nature "gave you an excellent body to reward love: which kind of liberal rewarding is crowned with an unspeakable felicity" (I, 379). Cecropia, moreover, sees marriage simply as a means of legitimizing this "unspeakable felicity." "What shall I say of the free delight, which the heart might embrace, without the accusing of the inward conscience, or fear of outward shame?" (I, 380). But the pleasure of which Cecropia speaks is all directed one way, toward the woman or, more precisely, toward herself. In this regard, it is not fundamentally different from the kind of passion experienced by Demagoras, who loves "nobody but himself, and for his own delight's sake Parthenia . . . " (I, 32). The same sort of egotism is reflected in Cecropia's praise of motherhood, for she sees children solely as "little models of yourself, [who] still carry you about them . . . " (I, 379).

In this, the first of several attempts to woo the princesses for Amphialus, Cecropia has laid down a value system that is totally egocentric; things and relationships are valuable because she prizes them or, what amounts to virtually the same thing, they give her pleasure. For her as for Shakespeare's Troilus, value is projected out from the self: "What is aught, but as 'tis valued?" (T&C, II, ii, 52). Cecropia's version of this mode of evaluation is even more difficult to counter than Troilus's: she makes no assertions about the nature of the world to which there may be factual or theoretical objections. Only her initial assumption about the source of value may be questioned, and that by proposing an alternative assumption. But there is no logical way to determine the relative validity of alternative assumptions. Opposition between axioms produces a logical impasse and the choice between them depends entirely (if one excludes the possibility of supernatural intervention in the matter) on the set of implications that the chooser wishes to develop.[9] The things and relationships valued in Cecropia's presentation are, albeit for different reasons, valued by Philoclea as well. Philoclea's experience with Pyrocles has taught her the importance of sexuality, she looks forward to her marriage to Pyrocles, and she in no way demonstrates an antipathy toward the idea of children. Because the implications of

Cecropia's argument are not radically different from Philoclea's own values, and because the initial assumption is
logically irrefutable, Philoclea has no choice but to remain
silent. She does so and in fact turns Cecropia's arguments
around by suggesting a way to add to their rhetorical force:
Philoclea

> only told her, that whilst she was so captived, she could not con-
> ceive of any such persuasions (though never so reasonable) any
> otherwise, than as constraints: and as constraints must needs even
> in nature abhor them, which at her liberty, in their own force of
> reason, might more prevail with her: and so fain would have re-
> turned the strength of Cecropia's persuasions, to have procured
> freedom. (I, 380-81)

Cecropia, then, begins the argument with a plea to reason,
" . . . if I speak reason, let reason have his due reward, persuasion" (I, 377); Philoclea ends the argument by moving it
to the proper ground for a conflict of assumptions, rhetoric,
and then wisely refuses to debate the issue. From Cecropia's
point of view, her confrontation with Philoclea has been
fruitless: the assertive motive fails to defeat natural innocence.

After this failure, Cecropia decides "to attempt Pamela,
whose beauty being equal, she hoped, if she might be won,
that her son's thoughts would rather rest on a beautiful gratefulness, than still be tormented with a disdaining beauty"
(I, 382). This move suggests the fault underlying Cecropia's
value structure. Focusing on beauty and sexual pleasure, and
resting at least part of her value system on transient qualities,
she cannot distinguish one beautiful woman from another.
Thus, because beauty is for Cecropia integrally related to
sexual pleasure, which she calls "love," her value system leads
logically to the kind of promiscuity practiced by Pamphilus
and Andromana. As these implications become clear, grounds
for debate with such a value system also become clear.

Cecropia has even less success with Pamela than she did with
Philoclea. Before she begins her attempt at persuading the
older sister to marry her son, she overhears Pamela's prayer,

which springs from a value system antithetical to Cecropia's. Turning outward from herself, Pamela places her destiny in the hands of a Christian-like God:

> my God, if in Thy wisdom, this be the aptest chastisement for my unexcusable folly; if this low bondage be fittest for my overhigh desires; if the pride of my not-enough humble heart, be thus to be broken, O Lord, I yield unto Thy will, and joyfully embrace what sorrow Thou wilt have me suffer. (I, 383)

It does not matter whether or not Sidney realized that in Pamela's prayer and in her subsequent debate with Cecropia he was siding with the "liberal" camp in the controversy concerning *prisca theologica*.[10] Even if Pamela's prayer and later argument were explicitly anti-Christian, which they are not, the value system implied would still be a contrast to Cecropia's. Pamela's submission to her God posits a source of value outside the self; it is explicitly nonegotistical. Any possible doubt that the *Arcadia* will vindicate Pamela's presuppositions is immediately dispelled by the "abashment at that goodness" (I, 383) that Cecropia feels after seeing Pamela become an image of devotion.

Cecropia's failures in verbal conflict, which result from her egotistical value system, are followed by the first military clash between Basilius and Amphialus. During the fighting Amphialus vainly attempts to act chivalrously, only to have his chivalry thwarted. In his combat with Agenor, who has left his beautiful face unprotected, for example, Amphialus's "compassion so rebated the edge of choler, that he spared that fair nakedness, and let his staff fall to Agenor's vamplate . . . " (I, 387). But this gesture is in vain: the shattered end of the lance slides up, "giving not only a sudden, but a foul death, leaving scarcely any tokens of his [Agenor's] former beauty . . . " (I, 387). This killing is, as Davis notes, characteristic of Amphialus's self-division.[11] To a large extent, Amphialus's self-division comes from his confusion of values; Agenor's gratuitous death is the direct result of that same confusion. The right arose out of Amphialus's complicity with Cecropia's plot and his unavoidable slaying of Agenor shows how any failure to oppose wickedness may render one ethically helpless — unable, like Amphialus, to evade the issue.[12]

This battle is gory; its violence and death are not glossed over by chivalric trappings or by some misplaced notion of the glory of death in war.

> The earth itself (wont to be a burial of men) was now (as it were) buried with men: so was the face thereof hidden with dead bodies, to whom death had come masked in divers manners. In one place lay disinherited heads, dispossessed of their natural seignories: in another, whole bodies to see to, but that their hearts wont to be bound all over so close, were now with deadly violence opened: in others, fouler deaths had uglily displayed their trailing guts. There lay arms, whose fingers yet moved, as if they would feel for him that made them feel: and legs, which contrary to common reason, by being discharged of their burden, were grown heavier. (I, 388)

The tone of this passage is unmistakable; it evokes revulsion for this display of "human inhumanity" (I, 10).[13] The grisly descriptions justify the phrase "contrary to common reason" and suggest how unnatural assertiveness may lead to war and to a confusion of values. By going along with Cecropia's plot, then, Amphialus has allowed, and perhaps even caused, an inversion of values; the effects of his love for Philoclea are not different from the effects of hate. This last inversion of attitudes, of love and hate, is made explicit when Musidorus, now disguised as the "black knight," confronts Amphialus: "as in two beautiful folks, Love naturally stirs a desire of joining, so in their two courages hate stirred a desire of trial" (I, 393).

iv

The combat between Musidorus and Amphialus is stopped by "an old governor of Amphialus, always a good knight, and

careful of his charge" (I, 393), who points out, when Amphialus complains that he has been dishonored by the intervention,
" . . . You say well . . . to stand now like a private soldier,
setting your credit upon particular fighting, while you may
see Basilius with all his host, is getting between you and your
town" (I, 393). Thus recalled into the public battle, Amphialus has retreat sounded, and the fighting is over for the day.
Amphialus immediately visits Philoclea and causes "his dream
to be sung unto her (which he had seen the night before he
fell in love with her) making a fine boy he had, accord a pretty
dolefulness unto it" (I, 394). The dream vision itself is something of a curiosity. Taken over from Philisides' autobiography
in the Fourth Eclogues of the *Old Arcadia*, it is, as Ringler
points out, "an adaptation of the well-known story of the
Judgement of Paris" (*Poems*, p. 418). But Amphialus gives
the judgment to the nymph, Mira, rather than to either of
the goddesses,[14] whose stature is noticeably diminished.

> But straight there issue'd forth two ladies (ladies sure
> They seemed to me) on whom did wait a virgin pure.
> Strange were the ladies' weeds; yet more unfit than strange.
> The first with clothes tucked up as nymphs in woods do range;
> Tuck'd up even with the knees, with bow and arrows press'd:
> Her right arm naked was, discovered was her breast.
> But heavy was her pace, and such a meagre cheer,
> As little hunting mind (God knows) did there appear.
> The other had with art (more than our women know,
> As stuff meant for the sale set out to glaring show)
> A wanton woman's face, and with curl'd knots had twin'd
> Her hair, which by the help of painter's cunning, shin'd.
> When I such guests did see come out of such house,
> The mountains great with child I thought brought forth a mouse.
> But walking forth, the first thus to the second said,
> "Venus come on": said she, "Dian you are obey'd."
> Those names abash'd me much, when those great names I heard:
> Although their fame (meseem'd) from truth had greatly jarr'd.
>
> (I, 396)

The reduction of the goddesses, surprising when set in an era
and locale believed to have been governed by those goddesses

among other deities, serves within the dream vision as a reason for preferring Mira over Venus and Diana. It may also rhetorically undercut pagan theology and thus enhance Pamela's doctrine prefiguring Christianity.

Amphialus's choice of Mira is ironically prompted by the discord between the goddesses:

> "How ill both you can rule, well hath your discord taught:
> Ne yet for ought I see, your beauties merit ought.
> To yonder Nymph therefore" (to Mira I did point)
> "The crown above you both for ever I appoint."
>
> (I, 398)

This decision invokes the wrath of the goddesses upon Amphialus:

> "Yet thou shalt not go free," quoth Venus, "such a fire
> Her beauty kindle shall within thy foolish mind,
> That thou full oft shall wish thy judging eyes were blind."
> "Nay then," Diana said, "the chasteness I will give
> In ashes of despair (though burnt) shall make thee live."
> "Nay thou," said both, "shalt see such beams shine in her face
> That thou shalt never dare seek help of wretched case."
> And with that cursed curse away to heaven they fled,
> First having all their gifts upon fair Mira spread.
>
> (I, 399)

The conflict between the fire given him by Venus and the chastity given, as he interprets the dream vision, to Philoclea is exactly what Amphialus feels in his courtship of the princess. Thus, the attempted resolution of the goddesses' discord produces in him exactly the same discord. Seeing Mira as an allegorical figure of Philoclea and so interpreting his dream as prophecy, his courtship is an attempt to work out the will of the very gods that the vision reduced in stature. But to act in any way on prophecy is, in the *Arcadia*, clearly faulty. This is clear from the consequences of Basilius's attempt to avoid the events predicted in the oracle and from the King of Phrygia's fruitless attempt to prevent the "after-expectations" prophesied at Musidorus's birth. These two examples are of characters trying to avoid predicted events; attempts to accord with predictions have similar results, as in Eschylus's belief "that he should die in the arms of his son" (I, 389) and Memnon's "that he should never be killed, but by his own companions" (I, 389), both of which prove true, but not in expected ways. Amphialus's prophetic dream, then, takes effect because Amphialus believes it; like all the other prophecies in the *Arcadia*, it is self-fulfilling.

After the poorly received recitation of his dream vision, Amphialus turns to the problem represented by Philanax, "whom he had not only long hated, but now had his hate greatly increased by the death of his squire Ismenus" (I, 399). Although Amphialus is unaware of it, his accidental slaying of Philanax's brother, Agenor, had directly caused the death of Ismenus. When Philanax encountered Ismenus during the battle, he was moved by the youth's beauty and "took pity of him; meaning to make him prisoner, and then to give him to his brother Agenor to be his companion, because they were not much unlike, neither in years, nor countenance" (I, 399). This compassion turned to revenge, however, when Philanax saw the mangled corpse of Agenor. The ambivalence of Amphialus's ethical stance, then, indirectly results in the death of Ismenus; the audience therefore repudiates Amphialus's reason for hating Philanax. Amphialus's second reason for planning the execution of Philanax is to rhetorically justify his claim that Basilius's viceregent was "one of the chief causes that moved him to this rebellion" and thus "color the better his action . . . " (I, 399). This politic rationalization suggests that Amphialus is now locked into a sequence he knows to be ethically wrong. He almost executes Philanax, but wavers at Philoclea's timely intervention. In acceding to Philoclea's request, "that if the love of her had any power of persuasion in his mind, he would lay no further punishment, than imprisonment, upon Philanax" (I, 400), however, Amphialus vacillates between Cecropia's value system and Philoclea's. To the degree to which he aligns himself with his mother, he is at fault; his wavering, however, indicates the accuracy of Philanax's remark, "Your fault passed is excusable, in that Love persuaded, and youth was persuaded" (I, 401). His culpability, then, is attenuated and still venial. He may still be forgiven if he follows Philanax's advice: "Do not urge the effects of angry victory, but rather seek to obtain that constantly by courtesy, which you can never assuredly enjoy by violence" (I, 401).

The confrontation between Cecropia and Pamela follows immediately. They hold firm and mutually exclusive value systems. Cecropia, still thinking that Pamela may prove a substitute for Philoclea in her son's affections, notices that Pamela, unlike Philoclea, had not "neglected the dainty dressing of herself . . . " (I, 403). Encouraged by this observation, Cecropia initiates her argument from beauty by complimenting Pamela's skill in embroidering a purse, and remarking that " . . . Full happy is he . . . at least if he knew his own happiness, to whom a purse in this manner, and by this hand wrought, is dedicated" (I, 403). Pamela disabuses her of the notion that she made the purse for someone or that she especially values it, claiming " . . . I promise you I wrought it, but to make some tedious hours believe, that I thought not of them: for else I valued it, but even as a very purse" (I, 403). This prompts Cecropia to claim that beauty often works "unwitting effects of wonder" (I, 403), to which Pamela replies that Cecropia overpraises beauty "since it is a thing, which not only beasts have; but even stones and trees many of them do greatly excell in it" (I, 403). But humans have the greatest potential beauty, argues Cecropia, because only they are able to perceive it. Beauty, moreover, is the special preeminence of women, who may use it to control men. "Men venture lives to conquer; she [*i.e.*, woman] conquers lives without venturing" (I, 404). If, in her dialogues with Philoclea, Cecropia stresses the pleasurable component of beauty, here she argues the power that results from beauty. She continually sees human relationships in terms of struggles in which one person is conquered and the other is a conqueror. Pamela quite rightly points out that in Cecropia's terms "these conquests . . . rather . . . proceed from the weakness of the conquered, than from the strength of the conquering power . . . " (I, 404) and that, even if love is therefore to be esteemed, one should not then suffer it to be defiled" (I, 404).

Cecropia claims to have no intention of defiling beauty. Quite the contrary, she intends to help Pamela to love because " . . . as colors should be as good as nothing if there were no eyes to behold them: so is beauty nothing, without the eye of Love behold it: and therefore, so far is it from defiling it, that it is the only honoring of it . . . " (I, 405). But Cecropia's belief that Pamela and Philoclea are interchangeable love-objects renders spurious this argument. Cecropia continues to equate love with sexual attraction — the product of beauty — and to assume that sexual attraction controls the minds of men. Thus she turns again to a *carpe diem* argument. The time is ripe and, once gone, cannot come again; Pamela, therefore, should not await parental consent and allow her "beauty to be hidden in the wrinkles of his [Basilius's] peevish thoughts" (I, 405). She should, in Cecropia's view, assert her own nature despite the lack of her father's approval. The princess's reply, " 'If he be peevish,' said Pamela, 'yet is he my father, and how beautiful soever I be, I am his daughter: so as God claims at my hands obedience, and makes me no judge of his imperfections' " (I, 405), suggests that she has attuned herself to an ordered universe and sees herself as a part within the whole of that universe. She can do no other than to deny the egotistical impulses suggested by, and represented in, Cecropia.

Pamela's argument centers on her concept of a hierarchical universe with a divine presence at its apex. Cecropia, realizing this, thinks that " . . . if she could make her less feeling of those heavenly conceits, that then she might easily wind her to her crooked bias" (I, 406). So she argues that clerks play on the fears of the common people; as Sidney elsewhere accuses lawyers of doing, religion "seeks to make men good, rather *formidine poenae*, then *virtutis amore* . . . " (III, 13).

Cecropia argues, however, that Pamela's intrinsic nobility sets
her apart; therefore " . . . I would not you should love virtue
servilely, for fear of I know not what, which you see not: but
even for the good effects of virtue which you see" (I, 406).
Since, Cecropia goes on, the origins of belief in the supernatural are in fear of the unknown and since " . . . all things
follow but the course of their own nature" (I, 406), it is folly
to ascribe a god to the universe. This kind of folly, moreover,
is characteristic only of man,

> who while by the pregnancy of his imagination he strives to things
> supernatural, meanwhile he loseth his own natural felicity. Be wise,
> and that wisdom shall be a God unto thee; be contented, and that
> is thy heaven: for else to think that those powers (if there be any
> such) above are moved either by the eloquence of our prayers, or in
> a chafe at the folly of our actions; carries as much reason as if flies
> should think, that men take great care which of them hums sweetest,
> and which of them flies nimblest. (I, 406-7)

Whether or not Lucretian atomic theory lies behind this doctrine,[15] Cecropia's closing statement, "Be wise, and that wisdom shall be a God unto thee . . . , " makes explicit the
blasphemous outer limits of Cecropia's egotism. It suggests
that the only constraints on the individual come from within
the self because there is no order intrinsic in the world.
Logically Cecropia's argument suggests that any value system
whatsoever can be acceptable. Since there are no checks,
other than possible goals, ethical relativism is not only viable,
it is mandatory; Pamphilus's behavior is neither better than,
nor worse than, Argalus's. Cecropia's argument, moreoever,
points the direction that a solipsistic theory of perception
might take and strongly suggests why Sidney was so careful
in Book I to give the world its due.

Pamela's reply to this argument shows her counterassumpt-
ions. The very order observed by Cecropia implies "that there
is a constancy in the everlasting governor" (I, 407). If, Pamela
argues, the world is eternal, it could not be governed by chance
because " . . . eternity, and chance are things unsufferable to-

gether" (I, 407). And if the world is not eternal, then it had a beginning and that beginning could not be by chance, since chance cannot create *ex nihilo*. And if there were substances on which chance could work, " . . . then those substances must needs have been from ever and so eternal: and that eternal causes should bring forth chanceable effects, is as sensible, as that the sun should be the author of darkness' (I, 408). The very nature of the world's constituent parts, Pamela continues, argues the intervention of a divine, guiding hand in creation, ". . . for their natures being absolute contrary, in nature rather would have sought each other's ruin, than have served as well consorted parts to such an unexpressible harmony" (I, 408). The diversity in unity seen everywhere in the world must be, then, the product of God's creation and control of the world. Such a God must of course be a reasonable God, for it would be the height of folly to think that rational, mortal man was created by a nonrational god. He, moreover, must have infinite knowledge and power and, because infinitely wise and powerful, must be infinitely good and just, " . . . for infiniteness of power, and knowledge, without like measure of goodness, must necessarily bring forth destruction and ruin, and not ornament and preservation" (I, 410). Finally, natural reason leads Pamela to the rhetorical crux of her argument, that this omnipotent and omniscient God is concerned with the affairs of man, and hence with Cecropia's evil:

> Since then there is a God, and an all-knowing God, so as He seeth into the darkest of all natural secrets, which is the heart of man; and sees therein the deepest dissembled thoughts, nay sees the thoughts before they be thought: since He is just to exercise His might, and mighty to perform His justice, assure thyself, most wicked woman (that has so plaguily a corrupted mind, as thou canst not keep thy sickness to thyself, but must most wickedly infect others) assure thyself, I say (for what I say depends of everlasting and unremovable causes) that the time will come, when thou shalt know that power by feeling it, when thou shalt see His wisdom in the manifesting thy ugly shamefulness, and shalt only perceive Him to have been a creator in thy destruction. (I, 410)

If Pamela hopes by this to frighten her aunt into releasing her prisoners, Cecropia's response must be a disappointment. Even so, Pamela manages to suggest that Cecropia's brand of egotism is fundamentally self-destructive. Cecropia's death later confirms Pamela's theological inference.

The debate between Cecropia and Pamela has certain interesting ramifications. While Pamela denies the basic tenets of Cecropia's value system, she does not deny all aspects. She is willing, for example, to accept, at least ironically, an excellency of beauty proposed by Cecropia. Neither niece argues that sex is not pleasurable. But the tenets Pamela accepts she accepts only in the framework of a more viable value system. Thus Pamela's value system incorporates the best aspects of Cecropia's value system but avoids its self-destructive quality. According to the criteria for appraising value systems, then, Pamela's is preferable since it maximizes rewards and minimizes punishments.

v

Amphialus's interview with Philoclea and Cecropia's with Pamela have focused on issues from the erotic theme. In the ensuing series of jousts, the emphasis shifts to public and political behavior, a shift marked by Basilius's preparations for a siege, encircling the town with trenches and building protective fortifications. These preparations confirm Philanax's report, "That he meant rather to win it by time, and famine, than by force of assault . . . " (I, 401). Basilius's pedestrian strategy indicates his greater concern with an efficient battle plan, and hence a successful conclusion to the war, than with the accumulation of personal glory.

The siege, however, is tedious and Phalantus, "his young spirits (weary of wanting cause to be weary) [desiring] to keep his valor in knowledge, by some private act, since the public policy restrained him . . . " (I, 412), sends a challenge to Amphialus. Characterized by a high degree of formality, the challenge is firmly rooted in the private values of a joust, " . . . liking of martial matters without any mislike of your person, . . . I desire to refresh my mind with some exercise of arms . . . " (I, 413), and so ignores the issue of the war. The *joie de vivre* of Phalantus, mistakenly directed earlier in defense of Artesia's beauty, is here clothed in the formal ritual of the chivalric code. The descriptions of Amphialus's and Phalantus's preparations for the combat stress the ritualistic quality. Phalantus arrays himself to be a showcase knight, and his armor, which is only slightly more elaborate than that of Amphialus, is not particularly designed for combat. The joust itself is, as the preparation for it would lead one to suspect, bloodless and ends after Amphialus strikes Phalantus "so cruel a blow on the knee, that the poor gentleman fell down withal in a swoon" (I, 417). The absurdity of this conclusion, particularly in the larger context of the siege, is not, moreover, attenuated by Phalantus's consolation that ". . . no balm could be more comfortable to his wound, than the knowledge thereof was to his mind, when he knew his mishap should be excused by the renowned valor of the other" (I, 418).

In spite of the touch of humor at the jousters' expense, the combat is rather attractive. This results partly from the youthful vitality manifested by both parties and partly from the separation of the joust from the larger war so that the joust is not touched by the kind of violence that characterizes the battle scenes. The difference between the private joust and the public war is significant, because the joust represents an idealized picture of combat while the battle scenes represent the reality of war. Hence, the contrast criticizes the idealization of war, especially in terms of glory to be gained, and shows the inadequacy of a chivalric code as a description of war. This corresponds, moreover, to the partial distance that is the rhetorical by-product of the comedy directed at Amphialus and Phalantus. The failure of the ideals of chivalry in the real world becomes more and more evident in the jousts that follow that of Amphialus and Phalantus. Although these begin in much the same spirit as the Amphialus-Phalantus combat, they degenerate to the indecisive joust between Amphialus and Musidorus that follows closely the death of Parthenia.

The progressive degeneration becomes evident as the Arcadian knights answer Amphialus's general challenge "that whatsoever knight would try the like fortune as Phalantus did, he should in like sort be answered . . . " (I, 419). These jousts are not bloodless, and Basilius grieves "so to see his rebel prevail, and in his own sight to crown himself with deserved honor" (I, 419-20). Within the larger context of the war, Amphialus substitutes heroism for strategy and risks far more than he can possibly gain,[16] as has been pointed out to him by the "old governor," who worries that Amphialus "would rather affect the glory of a private fighter, than of a wise general . . ." (I, 414). When the jousts become consciously connected with the war, moreoever, they become bloody. Thus, the combat of Amphialus and Phalantus implies a criticism of war precisely because it does not live up to the ideals of chivalry.

But Amphialus's victories over the Arcadian knights do affect the war: each victory increases Amphialus's power to attract followers at the same time as it depletes, if only in a small way, Basilius's forces. Out of respect for the recent marriage of Argalus and Parthenia, Basilius has earlier refrained from calling on that noble knight, "but now his honor, and (as he esteemed it) felicity standing upon it, he could no longer forbear to challenge of him his faithful service" (I, 420). The messenger sent by Basilius finds

> Argalus at a castle of his own, sitting in a parlor with the fair Parthenia, he reading in a book the stories of Hercules, she by him, as to hear him read; but while his eyes looked on the book, she looked on his eyes, and sometimes staying him with some pretty question not so much to be resolved of the doubt; as to give him occasion to look upon her. A happy couple, he joying in her, she joying in herself, but in herself, because she enjoyed him: both increasing their riches by giving to each other; each making one life double, because they made a double life one; where desire never wanted satisfaction, nor satisfaction ever bred satiety; he ruling, because she would obey: or rather because she would obey, she therein ruling. (I, 420)

This description of marital bliss shows the kind of marriage that grows out of the love shown earlier between Argalus and Parthenia. An example of the maximum potential of love, these two show the error of Musidorus's reasoning in his debate with Pyrocles.[17] The reintroduction of Argalus and Parthenia, moreover, reminds the audience of Argalus's fidelity in the face of Parthenia's disfigurement and so undercuts Cecropia's emphasis on physical beauty. The description of the couple's happiness also adds pathos to their deaths at the hands of Amphialus. As Davis puts it, "Argalus and Parthenia exemplify the ideal heroic marriage; but such a marriage is modified, by the context of the bloody heroic world, to tragedy."[18] But the force that destroys Argalus and Parthenia is not merely "the bloody heroic world," but heroic values turned to the bloody reality of war. Thus is Cecropia's selfishness allied with death against the life-forces represented in marriage.

Except for two crucial differences, the challenge sent to Amphialus by Argalus is almost as formal as that sent by Phalantus. In the first place, whereas Phalantus challenged Amphialus out of desire for personal glory and love of combat, Argalus's challenge is directly tied to the war. In the second place, Argalus's challenge is explicitly a mortal challenge. The joust itself corresponds to these differences in that it is bloodier and more violent than the earlier combat. Twice, when one of the combatants has his opponent at a disadvantage, he asks him to yield and receives a blow in return. These requests accord with the ritualistic quality, which differentiates joust from brawl. But when Argalus cuts through Amphialus's "shield, armor, and arm almost to the bone" (I, 425), "then Amphialus forgot all ceremonies, and with cruel blows made more of his [Argalus's] best blood succeed the rest . . . "(I, 425). The crux here is that "Amphialus forgot all ceremonies"; once the ceremonial distinction between joust and war is lost, the death of at least one of the knights is ensured. The Argalus-Amphialus joust, then, suggests not only the infectiousness of Cecropia's egotism — war's incursion into joust — but the destructive results of that infection — the bloody and pointless death of Argalus. Amphialus's victory does him no good even in the one realm in which he wants most to succeed, the courtship of Philoclea, for she is "ever sorriest, when he had best success . . . " (I, 428).

If the tainting of the joust by war leads to tragedy in the case of Argalus, it may also lead to the absurd, as in the "combat of cowards" (I, 434). The duel between Dametas and Clinias follows pretty much the pattern established in the earlier jousts, except that both participants are consummate cowards. Because Clinias has a deserved reputation for faintheartedness, " . . . Dametas began to think with himself, that if he made a challenge unto him, he would never answer it . . . " (I, 428), and but for Amphialus's intervention, Dametas would have been right. But Clinias does reply:

> Filthy drivel, unworthy to have thy name set in any letter by a soldier's hand written: could thy wretched heart think it was timorousness, that made Clinias suspend awhile his answer? No caitiff, no: it was but as a ram, which goes back to return with the greater force. Know therefore that thou shalt no sooner appear (appear now if thou darest) I say thou shalt no sooner appear in the island (O happy thou, if thou do not appear) but that I will come upon thee with all my force; and cut thee in pieces (mark what I say) joint after joint, to the eternal terror of all presumptuous villains. Therefore look what thou dost: for I tell thee, horrible smart, and pain shall be thy lot, if thou wilt needs be so foolish (I having given thee no such cause) as to meet with me. (I, 431)

This challenge surely parodies the challenges of Phalantus, Argalus, and Amphialus, particularly in the parenthetical "I having given thee no such cause." But where the earlier challenges and replies stress the virtue and valor of the opponent over those of the writer, Dametas's challenge and Clinias's reply stress the "virtue" and "valor" of the writer. Each tries to be bold, but only because each knows the other to be a coward: "These terrible words Clinias used, hoping they would give a cooling to the heat of Dametas his courage: and so indeed they did, that he did groan to hear the thundering of those threatenings" (I, 431).

Parody colors each aspect of this interlude; just as with the nobler knights, so Dametas must needs be armed.

> To this purpose many willing hands were about him, letting him have reins, peitrel, with the rest of the furniture, and very brave bases; but all coming from divers houses, neither in color nor fashion, showing any kindred one with another; but that liked Dametas the better: for that he thought would argue, that he was master of many brave furnitures. (I, 430)

The opportunities to yield given by Argalus and Amphialus to each other are similarly parodied when, having tripped his own horse with his lance and being protected from attack by the thrashing about of the fallen horse, Clinias rises,

> but so bruised in body, and broken in heart, that he meant to yield himself to mercy: and with that intent drew out his sword, intending when he came nearer, to present the pommel of it to Dametas. But Dametas, when he saw him come with his sword drawn, nothing conceiving of any such intent, went back as fast as his back and heels could lead him. (I, 433)

In addition to adding a complication to the basic plot — Clinias's eventual defeat at the hands of Dametas leads directly to his treachery against Amphialus and Cecropia — the "combat of cowards" serves to alleviate the gloom cast by the death of Argalus. This rhetorical function is suggested by the reason given for the urging that each member of Basilius's troop gives to Dametas in the challenge, "to ease his mind overcharged with melancholy . . . " (I, 429). The parodic sense of the interlude, moreover, shows comically the limitations of chivalric idealism: the ideals function according to the ability of men to make them function.[19] Thus, chivalric ideals can function well only when all the people involved are exceptionally good. Yet even essentially good people can be subverted by pride and egotism both of themselves and of others. The three jousts — Phalantus with Amphialus, Argalus with Amphialus, and Clinias with Dametas — present three perspectives on the relationship between chivalric ideals and the realities of war. Taken together, they stress the inapplicability of chivalry to war and they suggest that the full-blown egotism of Cecropia results not merely in the subversion of ideals but in the reality of tragedy or absurdity.

vi

Clinias's defeat especially discomfits him: " . . . though he wanted heart to prevent shame, yet he wanted not wit to feel shame; not so much repining at it for the abhorring of shame, as for the discommodities, that to them that are shamed, ensue" (I, 434-35). Finding "himself the scorning-stock of every company" and fearful of Basilius's punishment "if he did not redeem his former treason to Basilius, with a more treasonable falsehood toward Amphialus" (I, 435), Clinias and the malcontented Artesia plot to poison Amphialus and free the princesses. Artesia's complicity in Clinias's plot results directly from Cecropia's failure to kill the princesses, as she had promised, so that Artesia would be able to marry Amphialus. When, however, they broach the plot to Philoclea and Pamela, they are rebuffed by the princesses' virtue. Philoclea claims that " . . . she would rather yield to perpetual imprisonment, than consent to the destroying her cousin, who (she knew) loved her, though wronged her" (I, 438). Pamela, "(in whose mind virtue governed with the sceptre of knowledge) hating so horrible a wickedness, and straight judging what was fit to do" (I, 438), rejects the plot so loudly that Cecropia is apprised of the scheme and the plotters are apprehended. The motives of Cecropia and Artesia are essentially similar; each is driven toward self-destruction by pride and selfishness. The refusal of the princesses to go along with the escape plan, on the other hand, demonstrates their commitment to the virtues they have espoused in the debates with Amphialus and Cecropia. Their insistence on virtuous action, when to act treacherously would get them their freedom, shows that their antipathy to Cecropia's proposals does not stem primarily from the fact that each is already in love. It also shows how the sisters' values, in marked contrast to their aunt's, support life.

The disturbance within the castle is matched by the disturbances without when Anaxius, his brothers, and troop break through Basilius's lines to come to the aid of Amphialus. Anaxius shows the fullness of his power, "but the valiant, and faithful Philanax, with well-governed speed made such head against him, as would have showed, how soon courage falls in the ditch which hath not the eye of wisdom" (I, 440), except that Anaxius is saved by Amphialus. Anaxius's martial strength is, of course, a manifestation of totally unchanneled pride: he lacks concrete goals; even his friendship with Amphialus is completely the product of chance interpreted according to pride. Anaxius is what Pyrocles could become if he lacked self-control and so makes Pyrocles look the better for the contrast. Also, he has Cecropia's egotism without her direction of specific goals; his egotism is both more dangerous than Cecropia's in that it is unpredictable and less dangerous in that it tends to more rapid self-destruction.

Two most revealing aspects of Anaxius's character are his misogyny and his dislike of music. When Amphialus suggests that they visit the princesses, Anaxius egotistically demurs, claiming that women cannot help falling in love with him, "and I that in my heart scorn them as a peevish paltry sex, not worthy to communicate with my virtues, would not do you the wrong: since (as I hear) you do debase yourself so much as to affect them" (I, 441). This attack on women is a comic version of Musidorus's earlier misogyny, and suggests another consequence of Amphialus's self-conscious misbehavior. Earlier Amphialus began by deciding not to oppose his mother; now he must ally himself with another whose values he recognizes to be twisted. His complicity, then, continues to expand, until he finally elects to stand up for the values in which he believes.

Anaxius shows his dislike for music in responding to the song ostensibly played in his honor, but really meant for Philoclea's ears. "But Anaxius (seeming aweary before it was ended) told Amphialus, that for his part he liked no music, but the neighing of horses, the sound of trumpets, and the cries of yielding persons . . . " (I, 442). If the harmony of music is symbolic of harmonious order, whether in the macrocosm or in the microcosm, then Anaxius clearly stands for the antithesis of harmony, discord. This is borne out in the way he denigrates love, the harmonizer of man and woman.

When Anaxius is finally left in charge of Amphialus's castle, it is because Cecropia's plot moves toward culmination in Anaxius's unchained, discordant variety of selfishness.

The increased discord first manifests itself outside the castle. After the encounter in which Anaxius is treacherously wounded by one of Basilius's troop, "unworthy to have his name registered, since he did it cowardly, sideward, when he least looked that way . . . " (I, 444), Amphialus is challenged by the "Knight of the Tomb." The joust between the two is a strange and a sad affair. It begins with a tilt, aborted by Amphialus when he sees that the other has missed his rest. It then continues on the ground with the advantage going so much to Amphialus that he steps back and offers his opponent the opportunity to yield. His offer is summarily rejected and this so angers Amphialus that he, "redoubling his blows, gave him a great wound upon his neck, and closing with him overthrew him, and in the fall thrust him mortally into the body . . . " (I, 446). The "Knight of the Tomb" is revealed to be Parthenia, come to rejoin her dead husband. Her death finishes a pattern begun in Book I in which Argalus showed himself willing to die for her. Finally, her death exposes fully the image of destruction resulting from Cecropia's brand of egotism. Argalus's death, after all, occurs in the course of his occupation. Its tragic component, however, is emphasized by the death of his wife; we are finally left with the thought that, if Amphialus had only behaved according to the code of values he knew to be right, these tragedies need never have taken place.

Amphialus's reaction to what he has done is more powerful than any in Basilius's camp. He destroys his sword and quickly falls into self-pity, recalling "the mishaps of his youth, the evils he had been cause of, his rebelling with shame, and that shame increased with shameful accidents, the deaths of Philoxenus and Parthenia . . . " (I, 451). But he mistakes the cause of these misfortunes when he assumes that they result from his being "hated of the ever-ruling powers . . . " (I, 451) when, in fact, the responsibility for at least the death of Parthenia is his alone. It stems directly from his failure to act on the right difference between lust and love, as he explains that difference to his mother.

> Mother, Oh Mother, lust may well be a tyrant, but true love where it is indeed, it is a servant. Accursed more than I am, may I be, if ever I did approach her, but that I freezed as much in a fearful reverence, as I burned in a vehement desire. Did ever man's eye look through love upon the majesty of virtue, shining through beauty, but that he became (as it well became him) a captive? and is it the style of a captive to write, "Our will and pleasure"? (I, 451-52)

Had he put this doctrine into practice and freed his prisoners, Amphialus would have avoided the tragedies of Argalus and Parthenia. But he shares the responsibility for his mother's plot, which is advanced a step further when she counsels her son to rape Philoclea: " . . . Amphialus, know thyself a man, and show thyself a man: and (believe me upon my word) a woman is a woman" (I, 453).

Amphialus, however, has no chance to reply to his mother's suggestion — and it is unclear how he would have replied — because they are interrupted by yet another challenge. Although Amphialus tends "even to condemn himself, as though indeed his [the challenger] reproaches were true" (I, 454), his courage and anger force him to accept the challenge and he goes out to meet the "forsaken knight," who is, of course, Musidorus in disguise. The bloody battle between the two is, in a way, a paradigm of the jousts that have preceded it in spite of the fact that it is indecisive and ends with both combatants "lying immobilized on the field of magnanimity. . . ."[20] The battle begins with the usual courtesies, continues through a period in which the skill of the participants is stressed, and ends like a heavyweight boxing match with Amphialus and Musidorus standing and hacking at each other. Again the rules of formality give way to brutality. Amphialus, finally, is saved from death only through the unchivalric intervention of Anaxius's two brothers, and matters are not settled until troops from both sides arrive on the island to defend their fallen champions. The chaos Amphialus allowed by his refusal to act in accord with his own values has reached its apex. From here on, Amphialus is not directly involved in the action until he confronts his mother with her treachery and attempts suicide.

The individual combats have taken their toll on both the besiegers and the besieged. Amphialus "had such wounds, and gave such wounds to his mind, as easily it could not be determined, whether death or he made the greater haste one to the other . . . " (I, 464). The injuries that incapacitate Amphialus free Cecropia from the restraints of her son's virtue, and she plans, "now she had the government of all things in her own hands, to satisfy her son's love, by their yielding, or satisfy her own revenge in their punishment" (I, 465). First she tells Basilius to either lift the siege or watch his daughters being executed. With this demand, the degeneration of the situation resulting from Amphialus's refusal to act morally moves into its final stage, a stage of completely unchecked assertiveness. The opposing advice offered Basilius by Kalander and Philanax shows that neither of the alternatives proposed by Cecropia is tenable. Kalander supports lifting the siege on the grounds that the whole function of the siege was to free Pamela and Philoclea. Philanax, on the other hand, argues against lifting the siege:

> They threaten if you remove not, they will kill your daughters, and if you do remove, what surety have you, but that they will kill them, since if the purpose be to cut off all impediments of Amphialus his ambition, the same cause will continue when you are away. (I, 467-68)

Both arguments have their merits even if Philanax's is colder than Kalander's, for he is ready, if needs be, to risk the deaths of the princesses.[21] But Basilius does not base his final decision on either reason or his paternal love; instead he lifts the siege because he is "more careful for Zelmane, by whose besieged person, the poor old man was straightly besieged..." (I, 468). Thus, just when the chaos resulting from egotism is at its

height outside the castle, the audience is reminded of Basilius's share of responsibility by his irresponsible reason for
lifting the siege. From the "combat of cowards" through the
lifting of the siege, Arcadian affairs become more and more
disordered.

vii

Although chaos reaches its peak outside the castle with the
duel between Amphialus and Musidorus, there is more degeneration to come within the castle. Cecropia remains intent on
persuading one of the princess to marry Amphialus and on
poisoning the other.

> She resolving all extremities, rather than fail of conquest, pursued
> on her rugged way: letting no day pass, without new and new per-
> plexing the poor ladies' minds, and troubling their bodies: and still
> swelling, the more she was stopped, and growing hot with her own
> doings, at length, abominable rage carried her to absolute tyrannies,
> so that taking with her certain old women (of wicked dispositions,
> and apt for envy-sake to be cruel to youth and beauty) with a coun-
> tenance impoisoned with malice, flew to the sweet Philoclea, as if so
> many kites should come about a white dove, and matching violent
> gestures with mischievous threatenings, she having a rod in her hand
> (like a fury that should carry wood to the burning of Diana's temple)
> fell to scourge that most beautiful body. (I, 470-71)

The torturing of the princesses quickly grows to be something
more than a means of persuasion and becomes a pleasure in
itself. Cecropia's heart grows "not only to desire the fruit of
punishing them, but even to delight in the punishing them"
(I, 472). For Cecropia, then, one form of desirable sexual behavior is birching. Fortunately for the princesses, each has a
true lover, so each can bear up under Cecropia's tortures; here
again their values contrast with their aunt's.

The resistance of the princesses does nothing to alleviate
the assaults of Cecropia; indeed, it "made the poison swell in
her cankered breast, perceiving that (as in water) the more

she grasped the less she held . . . " (I, 474). The image of "poison . . . in her cankered breast" strikingly recalls Cecropia's earlier intent to "make Philoclea receive the poison [of Cecropia's value system] distilled in sweet liquor" (I, 376), and her continuing resolve of "cruelly intending the present impoisoning the one [of the princesses], as soon as the other's affection were purchased" (I, 469).[22] Now the image of poison has turned inward; the poison now feeds on Cecropia. Thus, the coalescence of Cecropia's norms and the image of poison shows the self-destructive aspect of egotistical values.

Because neither her plan to convince the princesses with "reason" nor her use of torture has persuaded either of her captives to marry her son, Cecropia decides that the "best way now was, that the one seeing indeed the other's death, should perceive, there was no dallying meant: and then there was no doubt, that a woman's soul would do much, rather than leave so beautiful a body" (I, 475). Cecropia, therefore, approaches Philoclea and tells her that " . . . she was now minded that one of their deaths should serve for an example to the other, that despising worthy folks was more hurtful to the despiser, than the despised . . . " (I, 475) and therefore " . . . she bade her prepare her eyes for a new play, which she should see within few hours in the hall of that castle" (I, 476). This threat does not dissuade Philoclea from her resolve not to marry Amphialus, however, " . . . since in herself she preferred death before such a base servitude, love did teach her to wish the same to her sister" (I, 475). Philoclea, moreover, is not only not tempted by Cecropia's threat, but offers herself in Pamela's place. This offer rhetorically convinces the audience that Philoclea's refusal to be moved by Cecropia's threat is not prompted by self-interest and so is additional confirmation of the superiority of the princesses' system of values. Although the beheading of Pamela[23] is a ruse, the audience is kept as much in the dark as the characters who watch the "execution." The audience thus stays internalized and so feels the same sense of "loss" as Philoclea and Pyrocles.

When the apparent execution fails to move Philoclea, Cecropia tries the same trick on Pamela. Pamela's reaction to her sister's "death" is not reported, however, and the audience views the event through Pyrocles' eyes. One morning, awakened by a noise, Pyrocles runs to a window and looks out to see the head of Philoclea in a bloody golden bowl, "having no veil, but beauty, over the face, which still appeared to be alive: so did those eyes shine . . . and sometimes . . . they moved . . . " (I, 483). The scene is a macabre one and works its effects through the contrast of the horrible death of Philoclea with the princess's natural beauty. Although there is a clue to the fact that Philoclea is not dead — it is an unusual corpse whose eyes move — the overwhelming impulse is to accept the grisly scene at face value just as Pyrocles does. His first reaction is to attempt suicide and with that intent " . . . he ran as hard as ever he could, with his head against the wall, with intention to brain himself: but the haste to do it made the doing the slower" (I, 483). Unlike Marlowe's Bajazeth and Zabina, in the first part of *Tamburlane*, Pyrocles stumbles and merely knocks himself unconscious. Upon regaining consciousness, he tempers his wish for suicide with the desire for revenge and so postpones any further attempts to take his own life.

Pyrocles' lament, which lasts "all that day and night" (I, 485), is interrupted by "a poor gentlewoman . . . that wish long life unto you" (I, 485). She offers consolation for what he has lost, but it is bitter to him and he wishes that he could have died rather than Philoclea. Pyrocles' bitterness is more than relieved by his discovery that the "poor gentlewoman" is "Philoclea, and as yet living: not murdered, as you supposed, and therefore be comforted" (I, 487). This discovery puts the consolation in a new light, which is made clear by Philoclea's remarks:

And so . . . I came stealing into your chamber: where (O Lord) what a joy it was unto me, to hear you solemnize the funerals of the poor Philoclea! That I myself might live to hear my death bewailed! And by whom? By my dear Pyrocles. That I saw death was not strong enough to divide thy love from me! (I, 489)

This gratification that Philoclea feels parallels Parthenia's when, restored by the skill of Helen's surgeon, she comes disguised to test Argalus's love and finds him faithful.

The parallel between this encounter between Pyrocles and Philoclea and the earlier one between Argalus and Parthenia is but one suggestion of the careful preparation for this episode. And the preparation is indeed necessary, for if the episode is extracted from the *Arcadia* — in the fashion of anthologies, as it were — several problems become immediately obvious. How, for example, is one to take Pyrocles' mourning, which Philoclea claims is excessive? And his plan for revenge, said to be a "yielding, in reason and manhood" (I, 483)? The legitimacy of Philoclea's testing Pyrocles' love has been established by the similar testing of Argalus by Parthenia in a less trying situation, but how does that affect the way in which the audience should take the consolation that she offers Pyrocles? Taking the episode in isolation, it is difficult to see how these questions can be answered, but the parallels between it and other episodes in the *Arcadia* provide answers. Thus, Pyrocles' mourning is at least partially justified by the similar and uncriticized mourning of Philoclea for Pamela and Argalus's for Parthenia, and his attempted suicide is rendered more acceptable when one recalls that Parthenia's suicide receives no negative comment. Pyrocles' mistake is in trying to commit suicide when Philoclea may still be alive — "the face, which still appeared to be alive" — and this is pointed out to him by the "poor gentlewoman": " 'And yet,' replied she, 'perchance Philoclea is not dead, whom you so much bemoan' " (I, 486). But even this fault is mitigated by Argalus's similar error when he killed Demagoras. Pyrocles' "yielding, in reason and manhood, . . . to destroy man, woman, and child, that were any way of kin to them that were accessory to this cruelty" (I, 483) shows how revenge is suspect in the *Arcadia*, and is a humanizing breach in his perfection not unlike the assault on Amphialus in the river scene.

Proper perspective shows that Philoclea's consolation is educative; but the lessons to be learned from it do not involve radical shifts in Pyrocles' behavior, only slight shifts. There are three crucial points in it. First, she points out that his Philoclea may be alive and so clearly differentiates Argalus's and Pyrocles' errors from Parthenia's error-free suicide; what might be appropriate behavior for Pyrocles if Philoclea is dead is totally inappropriate if she is alive. Second, Philoclea reminds Pyrocles — and the audience, for that matter — of the fact of death; the tragedy of Argalus and Parthenia lies not in their deaths, but in the manner of their deaths. Third, and most important, she points out that Pyrocles' mourning is at least partially selfish and, to that degree, it is faulty.

> "In truth," said she, "you would think yourself a greatly privileged person, if since the strongest building, and lastingest monarchies are subject to end, only your Philoclea (because she is yours) should be exempted. But indeed you bemoan yourself, who have lost a friend: you cannot her, who hath in one act both preserved her honor, and left the miseries of this world." (I, 486)

Thus Pyrocles' self-pity suggests that his attempted suicide is more in error than Parthenia's suicidal challenge of Amphialus. In spite of the necessarily fine line between them, Parthenia's plan to rejoin her husband differs in tone from Pyrocles' despairing attempt to leave "the miseries of this world." Parthenia's actions face up to the fact of death while Pyrocles' reject it.

The shift in emphasis resulting from Philoclea's consolation corresponds to a shift in the direction of the narrative. The latter turn is indicated both by the fact that Philoclea is able to visit Pyrocles and by the fact that Cecropia, although "with the same pity as folks keep fowl, when they are not fat enough for their eating" (I, 488-89), has allowed the sisters to meet with each other. Although Philoclea is unwilling to believe that this presages a change in their expectations, she reports to Pyrocles that this increase in freedom is due to Amphialus's intervention. While confined to his bed and recovering from the wounds received in the joust with Musidorous, he had warned his mother that he had "heard some inkling that we were evil intreated" and that if Philoclea "received further hurt than the want of . . . liberty, he would not live an hour longer" (I, 489). Upon recovery and after being rebuffed by Pamela and Philoclea, Amphialus "straight by threatening torture, learned of one of the women, in what terrible manner those princesses had been used" (I, 492). Thus the full consequences of his acquiescence are finally manifested to him and he rushes to Cecropia, planning to kill himself while she watches. His wicked mother, however, misconstrues his motives and, fearing for her life, backs over the edge of the roof. As she dies, she confesses her plans to "Impoison the princesses, and would then have had them murdered. But everybody seeing, and glad to see her end, had left obedience to her tyranny" (I, 492). Her death results directly from her attribution to Amphialus of the sort of motive that she herself would have had.

Although the discovery of his mother's total depravity leads Amphialus to an existential awareness of responsibility, his self-conception remains inauthentic.[24] Although his decision to commit suicide may result partly from the discovery of his mother's perfidy and his own guilt, it also stems from his sense of being constrained by fate.

"And was I not enough miserable before," said he, "but that before my end I must be the death of my mother? Who how wicked soever, yet I would she had received her punishment by some other. O Amphialus, wretched Amphialus; thou has lived to be the death of thy most dear companion and friend Philoxenus, and of his father, thy most careful fosterfather. Thou has lived to kill a lady with thine own hands, and so excellent, and virtuous a lady, as the fair Parthenia was: thou hast lived to see thy faithful Ismenus slain in succoring thee, and thou not able to defend him: thou has lived to show thyself such a coward, as that one unknown knight could overcome thee in thy lady's presence: thou hast lived to bear arms against thy rightful prince, thine own uncle: thou hast lived to be accounted, and

> justly accounted, a traitor, by the most excellent persons that this world holdeth: thou hast lived to be the death of her, that gave thee life. But ah wretched Amphialus, thou hast lived for thy sake, and by thy authority, to have Philoclea tormented: O heavens, in Amphialus' castle, where Amphialus commanded; tormented, tormented? Torment of my soul, Philoclea tormented: and thou hast had such comfort in thy life, as to live all this while. (I, 492-93)

In this self-pity there is recognition of guilt but not of the freedom of individual action, and the latter is the mark of authentic existence. "The authentic person has really decided. He is sure of the whole of himself as revealed in the light of his last possibilities. He knows that his being is not circumscribed like that of a thing, not locked up inside of a mind container."[25] Amphialus's decision to kill himself, like Pyrocles' earlier attempt, is inauthentic precisely because it is but another retreat from responsibility, from the overwhelming burden of guilt. Had the *Arcadia* been completed, the attempt might have marked a major turning point in the life of Amphialus. Although his self-inflected injuries are regarded as mortal by the physicians who treat him under Anaxius's command, Helen of Corinth arrives with a special treatment and takes him to be cared for by the physician who worked the wondrous cure on Parthenia. But the oracle is silent on his further adventures.

viii

With Cecropia dead and Amphialus seriously wounded, Anaxius is left in charge of the castle. Distraught, and "his mind apter to revenge, than tenderness" (I, 503), he instructs his brothers to keep the prisoners safe while he conveys Helen to Corinth, and "to tell them this courteous message: that at his return with his own hands; he would cut off their heads, and send them for tokens to their father" (I, 503). This adds to the error of Amphialus's suicide attempt, for it results in putting Philoclea back into exactly the kind of danger that Cecropia had threatened. Anaxius's "courteous message" looks forward as well; what follows is a comic version of the captivity episode. The comic aspects of this portion are first indicated by the narrator's report that Musidorus "was bringing force, by force to deliver his lady" (I, 504). Shortly before the attempted rape of the ladies, moreover, " . . . Anaxius had word, that from the tower there were descried some companies of armed men, marching towards the town . . ." (I, 511). The import of this is to justify Pyrocles' continuing hope "that Musidorus would find some means to deliver them . . ." (I, 512) and Pamela's remark that ". . . only Musidorus, my shepherd, comes between me and death, and makes me think I should not die, because I knew he would not I should die" (I, 504). For the first time during the captivity episode the audience has firm expectation of a rescue by Musidorus. The absence of such expectancy elsewhere in Book III adds force to hope here and reduces the tension the audience might otherwise feel at Anaxius's threat. Tension is similarly released by the unambiguous oracular message that Basilius should "deny his daughters to Anaxius and his brothers, for that they were reserved for such as were better beloved of the Gods. That he should not doubt, for they should return unto him safely and speedily" (I, 510). Thus, unlike the part of the captivity episode dominated by Cecropia, the remaining portion must be read in light of these assurances that all will be well.

The comic assurances of this episode match the heavy emphasis on the humor in Anaxius's situation; the prideful warrior no sooner goes "into the chamber, where they were all three together; with full intention to kill the sisters with his own hands" (I, 504), when he is erotically attracted to Pamela. The very idea that Anaxius, who "in my heart scorn them [women] as a peevish paltry sex, not worthy to communicate with my virtues" (I, 441), should lust after the noble, majestic Pamela is ludicrous, as is his ensuing gentle courtship: "And withal, going to Pamela, and offering to take her by the chin, 'And as for you, minion,' said he, 'yield but

gently to my will, and you shall not only live, but live so
happily' " (I, 506-7). He shows his vanity again when he
chooses, as messenger to Basilius, "an officious servant
(whom he esteemed very wise, because he never found him
but just of his opinion)" (I, 509) and yet again in his ready
acceptance of his servant's negative report: Basilius has been
informed by the Delphic oracle "that he should not presume
to marry his daughters, to one who already was enrolled
among the demigods, and yet much less he should dare the
attempting to take them out of his hands" (I, 511). This
quality of the absurd reaches its peak as Zoilus advances on
"Zelmane,"

> smacking his lips, as for the prologue of a kiss, and something ad-
> vancing himself, "Darling," said he, "let thy heart be full of joy, and
> let thy fair eyes be of counsel with it, for this day thou shalt have
> Zoilus, whom many have longed for; but none shall have him, but
> Zelmane. And oh! how much glory I have to think what a race will
> be between us. The world, by the heavens, the world will be too
> little for them." (I, 513)

Pyrocles tries a ruse to get a sword for himself by claiming
that he made a vow "among my countrywomen, the famous
Amazons, that I would never marry none, but such one as
was able to withstand me in arms . . . " (I, 513). But the
ruse fails and

> Zoilus (but laughing with a hearty loudness) went by force to em-
> brace her; making no other answer, but since she had a mind to try
> his knighthood, she should quickly know what a man of arms he
> was: and so, without reverence to the ladies, began to struggle with
> her. (I, 513)

If Zoilus had been successful in his struggle, he would have
been rather surprised, but Pyrocles trips him, takes his sword
away, and, after a brief chase, " . . . she hit him with his own
sword, such a blow upon the waist, that she almost cut him
asunder: once, she sundered his soul from his body, sending it

to Proserpina, an angry goddess against ravishers" (I, 513-14). After killing Zoilus, Pyrocles fights and kills Lycurgus, and the revision ends in the midst of the fight between Pyrocles and Anaxius.[26]

Although Book III is incomplete, certain conclusions may be drawn from its heavy emphasis on the problem of value. Throughout the course of the book, two basic and radically different value systems are tested against one another. On the one hand, we have the values proposed by Cecropia and acted out, among the major characters, by Cecropia and Anaxius. These values are fundamentally egocentric and, because they depend entirely upon the individual's desires, lead philosophically to ethical relativism and pragmatically to self-destruction. Opposed to egotistical values are the more outward-looking values of Pamela, Philoclea, Pyrocles, Musidorus, Argalus, and Parthenia. The key to these is the recognition of the fundamentally ordered universe governed by both physical and moral laws. The source of the order appears to be the providence of the gods, most obviously manifested through the oracles.

Even if the oracles are the gods' mode of intervening in the world, the unresolved difference in clarity between the first and second presents problems. Nonetheless, I may suggest that Basilius's first contact with the oracle smacks of Cecropia's egotism and hence the oracle is ambiguous. But the oracle sent in reply to Basilius's question whether his daughters should marry Anaxius and Lycurgus is perfectly unambiguous and suggests that the universe of the *Arcadia* is ultimately in the hands of the gods. Reading backwards, then, I can go on to suggest that the first oracle was a device of the gods to cause exactly what has happened in the main plot of the first three books of the *Arcadia*. And its ambiguity is a reminder that the gods' purposes are shrouded in mystery revealed at the will of the gods but not to be penetrated by man.

Man, this book suggests, must accommodate himself to the fact of a moral code outside himself and do his best to live by it. He cannot, however, assume full knowledge of the code in the manner of Philanax's advice to Basilius, for that is a presumption of godlike powers and courts disaster. More than recognition is required, as Amphialus's behavior shows. One must act morally or one allows evil to spread. Finally, Pamela's wavering shows how easy it is to misconstrue the order of the universe. Faced with Anaxius's threat, she exclaims,

> And why . . . shall we any longer flatter adversity? Why should we delight to make ourselves any longer balls to injurious fortune . . . ? As for me, and my sister, undoubtedly it becomes our birth to think of dying nobly, while we have done, or suffered nothing, which might make our souls ashamed at the parture from these bodies. Hope is the fawning traitor of the mind, while under color of friendship, it robs it of his chief force of resolution. (I, 508)

But to give up hope is to forget that benign order for which Pamela argued so eloquently in her debates with Cecropia. To contemplate suicide, and this is the direction in which her exclamation is moving, before all possibilities are exhausted is to give up on the gods. Pyrocles argues from his new-found knowledge the better way:

> But yet the time (which ought always to be one) is not tuned for it [death]; while that may bring forth any good, do not bar yourself thereof: for then will be the time to die nobly, when you cannot live nobly. (I, 508)

The position at which Pyrocles has arrived is, in its own way, the resolution of conflict of values and will get another spokesman in *Hamlet*:

> we defy augury: there's a special providence in the fall of a sparrow. If it be now, 'tis not to come; if it be not to come, it will be now; if it be not now, yet it will come: the readiness is all. (V, ii, 230-34)

Notes

1. Even Davis, convinced as he is that the *Arcadia* is a demonstration of

Ficino's Neoplatonism, suggests the importance of normative issues as legitimate subjects of inquiry in the *Arcadia* when he notes that the Pamela-Cecropia debate on atheism moves "in an orderly fashion from the initial practical question of marriage to theoretical questions of autonomy and the nature of the universe" (*A Map of Arcadia*, p. 127). Incidentally, Davis may spend less time on the portion of Book III of the revision that Sidney had completed before his death than on the other portions of the *Arcadia* because for him the question of value is resolved through the use of Ficino.

2. Even so, much of what Sidney deals with in Book III is doctrinal and has analogues in philosophic and religious treatises of the Renaissance and earlier. Hence much of the criticism dealing with Book III has concerned itself primarily with the question of sources and analogues. Studies of this sort include: Ronald Levinson, "The 'Godlesse Minde' in Sidney's *Arcadia*," *MP* 29 (1931): 21-26; Constance M. Syford, "The Direct Source of the Pamela-Cecropia Episode in the *Arcadia*," *PMLA* 49 (1934): 472-89; D. P. Walker, "Ways of Dealing with Atheists: A Background to Pamela's Refutation of Cecropia," *BHR* 17 (1955): 252-77; Angelo M. Pellegrini, "Bruno, Sidney, and Spenser," *SP* 40 (1943): 128-44.

3. As Davis points out, " 'Amphialus' means 'between two seas,' and this name is emblematic of his spiritual vacillation; without a clear sense of right, he becomes a pipe for others to play on" (*A Map of Arcadia*, p. 131).

4. See *Astrophil and Stella*, sonnet 12, for example (*Poems*, pp. 170-71).

5. The rhetorical effectiveness of Amphialus's attack on Philanax has been prepared for in the unrest reported by Kalander in Book I (I, 26).

6. The comma in "coolness, to deal violently" is clearly rhythmic rather than syntactic, so that the sense of "coolness, to deal violently" is "coolness toward dealing violently." This reading is dictated by the context that deals with Amphialus's success with the rhetoric of his justification.

7. Cecropia's egotism is frequently shown by her attitude toward her relationship with the gods. Thus "Did I go to church? It seemed the very gods waited for me, their devotions not being solemnized till I was ready" (I, 364). Likewise, her first plot to destroy Basilius is aborted " . . . when the heavens (I think envying my great felicity) then stopped thy father's breath . . . " (I, 364).

8. This slight equivocation on Philoclea's part — she did, after all, make such a vow before she and Pyrocles exchanged mutual pledges of love — is surely permissible in light of the situation in which she finds herself.

9. Mathematicians are, of course, well aware of this phenomenon. A set theory that accepts the axiom of choice, for example, is radically different from one that does not. Both are, moreover, sound.

10. William R. Elton, "*King Lear* and the Gods" (San Marino, 1966), p. 41. See also D. P. Walker's article, pp. 254-55, 276-77.

11. *A Map of Arcadia*, p. 132.

12. Amphialus's complicity with Cecropia's plot is much like Albany's early lack of commitment in *King Lear*. And like Amphialus, Albany's passivity throughout the first half of the play renders him incapable of effective moral action until he makes his commitment in IV, ii.

13. Robert Kimbrough uses the sort of tone found in this passage as well as elsewhere in Book III as evidence for a fundamental shift in Sidney's attitude toward his work. This shift, he suggests, surprised Sidney and prevented Sidney's completion of the *New Arcadia*. Kimbrough goes on to say, "If Sidney had remained an artist, the logical step for him to have taken was to the novel proper" (p. 142). The difficulty is, of course, that Kimbrough overstates the shift; the description of the shipwreck in Book I (I, 9-10), for all its pictorial qualities, has a similar tone.

14. Amphialus's decision to award the judgment to Mira is, of course, analogous to the decision made by Diana in Peele's *The Arraignment of Paris* (published 1584). Although the chronological relationship between the *Old Arcadia* and Peele's play is less than certain, the most likely line of influence, if there is one at all, is from Sidney to Peele. A far safer assumption, however, is that both authors drew from a common tradition that would include the pageant performed at the coronation of Anne Boleyn (1533) (Douglas Bush, *Mythology and the Renaissance Tradition in English Poetry*, rev. ed. [New York, 1963], pp. 80-81). Ringler remarks, relevant to this matter, "See the epigram on the actress Ariadne in the Greek Anthology (v. 222), which says that if there were a new contest for beauty, Venus would lose because Paris would revise his judgement in favour of Ariadne" (*Poems*, p. 418).

15. If such matters are to be settled by consensus, Greenlaw's claim for Lucretius ("The Captivity Episode," pp. 59-62) is the preferred one. Nonetheless, Levinson argues against Lucretius and for Cicero's *De natura deorum* as the primary source, although, "In courtesy we may allow a certain dwindling residuum of" Lucretian elements (p. 26). Constance Miriam Syford, on the other hand, argues for Plutarch's *Moralia* as the major source, but she admits other influences as well. "These other influences are, in my conviction, Lucretius and Cicero, but Du Plessis Mornay least, if at all" (p. 488). The sense one receives from these various studies and arguments is that the issues debated by Pamela and Cecropia were very much alive in the sixteenth and seventeenth centuries and that, therefore, Sidney could have gone to any of a multitude of philosophic and theological debates for material to use in his fictional debate. This sense is confirmed by the plurality of references cited in Don Cameron Allen's *Doubt's Boundless Sea: Skepticism and Faith in the Renaissance* (Baltimore, 1964) and in D. P. Walker's article. Finally, to anticipate a little, Pamela's reply to Cecropia bears a marked resemblance to one of the arguments used by Aquinas in demonstrating the existence of God.

16. See, in this regard, Myrick's discussion of martial matters (pp. 256-58).

17. Mark Rose puts it this way: "Musidorus' error is that he makes no satisfactory distinction between love and lust. All love of woman is lust to him, and there is no provision in his philosophy for such admirable, though earthly, lovers as Argalus and Parthenia (*Heroic Love*, p. 48).

18. *A Map of Arcadia*, p. 130.

19. Many of these points are also made in Waldo F. McNeir's useful article, "Trial by Combat in Elizabethan Literature," *Die Neueren Sprachen* 15 (1966): 106. The absurd joust between Dametas and Clinias is similar to the one found later between Viola-Cesario and Sir Andrew in *Twelfth Night* and may indeed be the source for it (Pyle, pp. 449-50).

20. *A Map of Arcadia*, p. 134.

21. Assuming that the trial of the princes in Act V of the *Old Arcadia* (IV, 348-87) would have been taken over essentially unchanged for the revised *Arcadia*, Philanax's harsh advise to Basilius here anticipates and suggests the limitations of Philanax's later cold concern for justice untempered by mercy, for law and order rather than justice.

22. This is the second explicit reference to Cecropia's plan to poison the princess who does not accept Amphialus as soon as the other does. See also I, 401.

23. Wolff argues that the direct source for the pretended executions is the *Clitophon and Leucippe* of Achilles Tatius (pp. 316-17); see his summary of similar incidents in the Greek romance, pp. 60-63, 72-73, and 107-8).

24. The term *inauthentic* and its converse, *authentic*, are borrowed from existentialism and can be found explained in detail in any good primer of that philosophy, among which John Wild's *The Challenge of Existentialism* (Bloomington, Ind., 1955; 1966) is as good as any. Perhaps Heidegger's *Sein und Zeit*, available in an English translation by John Macquarrie and Edward Robinson (New York, 1962) is the most representative of the primary works that deal with the problem of authenticity.

25. Wild, p. 129.

26. Although the text breaks off, the final sentence and a half suggest that Pyrocles would have had the victory. "But Zelmane strongly putting it by with her righthand sword, coming in with her left foot, and hand, would have given a sharp visitation to his right side, but that he was fain to leap away. Whereat ashamed (as having never done so much before in his life) . . . " (I, 519). Thus Pyrocles is doing a better job of fighting than any of Anaxius's earlier foes.

5

Conclusion

The *New Arcadia* breaks off in mid-sentence and we shall
probably never know why. Either Sidney's political duties
and death prevented him from finishing the work, or he vol-
untarily gave it up as a lost cause. The former explanation is
the older one; the latter has been advanced lately with increasing force and with several justifications. On the one hand,
Sidney's revision may have made his original plan unworkable;
on the other hand, the shift in tone between the *Old Arcadia*
and the *New* may have become so pronounced that Sidney
"quit writing in disgust."[1] I cannot accept either of these
newer theories. The foregoing analysis suggests a work that
is architectonically sound, although radically different in kind

186

from its immediate predecessor.[2]

Let me sum up the arguments. First, the audience is consistently internalized. Although the narrator in the *New Arcadia* is omniscient, the point of view tends to be restricted to the character on whom the narrative is focused at any given moment. This has two specific effects. When the audience's knowledge of events is the same as the characters', the audience tends to accept the value system of the protagonists and so to sympathize with them. Sometimes, of course, the narrative deviates from this pattern — for example, when the point of view shifts from one character to another, giving the audience an edge in knowledge over the character newly in focus. Such deviations increase sympathy, or alleviate the tension that might otherwise create undesirable anxiety. The prime example of one kind of shift is, of course, the narrator's intrusion in Book II to introduce Philoclea's love complaint. This intrusion, however, further internalizes the audience and increases sympathy for Philoclea as it alleviates the tension that might otherwise detract from the audience's sense of her. Similarly, throughout Book II the audience is aware, while Musidorus is not, that Pamela returns his love. This allays tension and so increases the comic enjoyment of the prince's plight. Yet another shift to the same effect occurs during the captivity episode in Book III. The audience always knows more than the evil characters, especially concerning the princesses' feelings, and is therefore able to observe Cecropia's machinations and Amphialus's confusions with little worry about the outcome.

Second, Sidney holds in balance throughout the *New Arcadia* the demands of the erotic theme and the political theme. He produces, moreover, significant variations in both categories. The erotic stories include not only the idealized loves of Pyrocles, Musidorus, Argalus, and others, but vicious varieties of the erotic drive, as represented by Andromana and Pamphilus, comic versions of eroticism like the passions of Basilius and Gynecia, and exceptionally complex erotic entanglements like those which revolve about Amphialus. In the political sphere, there are not only the admirable rulers, such as Euarchus and Helen of Corinth, and evil rulers, such as the old Kings of Pontus and Phrygia, but also varying degrees of ineptitude in government, running from Basilius and the *"Paphlagonian* unkind King" to Plangus's father, the King of Iberia. Sidney, moreover, balances the demands of the two themes. He recognizes, and credits as important, both physical desire and more elevated forms of love. He credits both the privileges and the responsibilities of rulers: though the populace has an obligation to the ruler, the ruler has obligations also, obligations abandoned by Basilius in his pastoral retreat. Sidney, moreover, avoids making his two themes irreconcilable or even disjunctive categories; in the *New Arcadia*, they are interrelated. If Erona's love for the base Antiphilus leads to political strife among some nations, Amphialus's love of Philoclea finally checkmates Cecropia's political ambitions and establishes the situation in which the Arcadian revolt can be ended.

Although the *New Arcadia* must be called idealistic, if only because it postulates the existence of such nearly perfect characters as Euarchus, Pyrocles, Musidorus, Argalus, Philoclea, Pamela, and Parthenia, the idealism it promulgates is not absolutistic. Sidney recognizes, and gives credence, not only to alternate conceptions but to the view that man is an imperfect creature living in a fallen world. This last is particularly borne out in the plurality of forces operating on the characters and in the complexity of the ethical decisions they are forced to make, all of which is manifested in the complexity of the narrative structure.

The double concern of the *New Arcadia* — eros and civilization — suggests that the work is expansive in its implications. Put otherwise, the *New Arcadia* deals with human behavior in a very broad sense, instead of restricting itself to one narrow aspect. Thus Fulke Greville can emphasize the political lesson when he claims that Sidney's intent, and scope was, to turn the barren Philosophy precepts into pregnant Images of life; and in them, first on the Monarch's part, lively to represent the growth, state, and declination of Princes, change of Government, and lawes: visissitudes of sedition, factions, succession, confederacies, plantations, with all other errors, or alterations in publique affaires. Then again in the subjects case; the state of favor, prosperitie, adversity, emulation, quarrell, undertaking, retiring, hospitality, travail, and all other modes of private fortunes, or misfortunes.[3]

Sir William Alexander, on the other hand, praises the work for the private virtues it promulgates:

But I confess that the *Arcadia* of S. P. *Sidney* (either being considered in the whole or in several Lineaments) is the most excellent Work that, in my Judgment, hath been written in any Language that I understand, affording many exquisite Types of Perfection for both Sexes; leaving the Gifts of Nature, whose Value doth depend upon the Beholders, wanting no Virtue whereof a Humane Mind could be capable: as for Men, Magnanimity, Carriage, Courtesy, Valour, Judgment, Discretion; and in Women, Modesty, Shamefastness, Constancy, Continency, still accompanied with a tender sense of Honor.[4]

Surely Alan D. Isler is right in asserting that "there is no need to attempt to resolve the dispute between Sir Fulke Greville and Sir William Alexander, for it is more apparent than real."[5] The *New Arcadia* can accommodate both the political and moral philosopher, precisely because their views are simply two perspectives on human behavior, besides being the thematic centers of the *New Arcadia*.

Third, Sidney's manner of structuring his narrative reflects the breadth of his thematic concerns rather than oversimplifying them. Even today events may be seen as taking place in space, in time, and within a structure of values. But neither in the *New Arcadia* nor in the world are these three structures wholly distinct. Movement in space entails movement in time and conversely. And since problems of value are finally resolved by the consequences of ethical decisions, a temporal perspective is required for a normative one. The interrelated structures of the narrative are interrelated ways of viewing human behavior — both erotic and political. And the *New Arcadia*, although idealistic, is neither flat nor simplistic. Unless human behavior has changed radically in the last four hundred years, Sidney's work has much to say to a modern audience.

Notes

1. Kimbrough, p. 142. Other adherents of the theory of abandonment include Lanham (*The Old "Arcadia"*), Elizabeth Dipple ("Metamorphosis in Sidney's *Arcadias.*" PQ 50 [1971], 47-62 and "The Captivity Episode and the *New Arcadia" JEGP* 70 [1971]), Lindheim ("Vision, Revision").

2. A similar view is expressed by Lawry, p. 166.

3. Greville, pp. 15-16.

4. *Anacrisis* (1634?) in *Critical Essays of the Seventeenth Century*, ed. J. E. Spingarn (Oxford, 1957; Bloomington, Ind., 1963), 1: 187.

5. "Moral Philosophy," p. 360.

Editions of Sidney

Sidney, Sir Philip. *The Countess of Pembroke's "Arcadia."* Facsimile of 1590 Quarto Edition. Edited by H. Oskar Sommer. London, 1891.

    The Countess of Pembroke's "Arcadia." Facsimile of 1590 Quarto Edition. Edited by Carl Dennis. Kent, Ohio, 1970.

    The Prose Works of Sir Philip Sidney. Edited by Albert Feuillerat. Cambridge, England, 1962.

    The Poems of Sir Philip Sidney. Edited by William A. Ringler, Jr. Oxford, 1962.

    Old Arcadia. Edited by Jean Robertson. Oxford, 1973.

Select Bibliography

Allen, Don Cameron. *Doubt's Boundless Sea: Skepticism and Faith in the Renaissance*. Baltimore, Md., 1964.

Anderson, D. M. "The Dido Incident in Sidney's 'Arcadia.' " *N&Q* n.s. 3, 201 (1956): 417-19.

Brie, Friedrich. *Sidney's "Arcadia": Eine Studie zur Englischen Renaissance*. Strasburg, 1918.

Bush, Douglas. *Mythology and the Renaissance Tradition in English Poetry*. Rev. ed. New York, 1963.

Buxton, John. *Elizabethan Taste*. New York, 1964.

Campbell, Lily Bess. *Divine Poetry and Drama in Sixteenth-Century England*. Berkeley, Calif., 1959.

Cassirer, Ernst. *The Philosophy of Symbolic Forms*. Translated by Ralph Manheim. 3 vols. New Haven, Conn., 1953; 1968.

Challis, Lorna. "The Use of Oratory in Sidney's *Arcadia*." *SP* 62 (1964): 561-76.

Danby, John F. *Elizabethan and Jacobean Poets: Studies in Sidney, Shakespeare, Beaumont and Fletcher*. London, 1952; 1965.

Davis, Walter R. "Thematic Unity in the *New Arcadia*." *SP* 57 (1960): 123-43.

———. "Actaeon in Arcadia." *SEL* 2 (1962): 95-110.

———. *A Map of "Arcadia," Sidney's Romance in Its Tradition*, in *Sidney's Arcadia*. YSE 158. New Haven, Conn., 1965.

———. *Idea and Act in Elizabethan Fiction*. Princeton, N. J., 1969.

Delasanta, Rodney. *The Epic Voice*. The Hague, 1967.

Dipple, Elizabeth. "The 'Fore Conceit' of Sidney's Eclogues." *Literary Monographs* 1. Madison, Wis., 1967.

———. "Harmony and Pastoral in the *Old Arcadia*." *ELH* 35 (1968): 309-28.

———. " 'Unjust Justice' in the *Old Arcadia*." *SEL* 10 (1970): 83-101.

———. "The Captivity Episode and the *New Arcadia*." *JEGP* 70 (1971): 418-31.

———. "Metamorphosis in Sidney's *Arcadias*." *PQ* 50 (1971): 47-62.

Duhamel, P. Albert. "Sidney's *Arcadia* and Elizabethan Rhetoric." *SP* 45 (1948): 134-50.

Duncan-Jones, Katherine. "Sidney's Urania." *RES* n.s. 17 (1966): 123-32.

Elton, William R. *"King Lear" and the Gods*. San Marino, Calif., 1966.

Erikson, Erik. *Childhood and Society*. 2d ed. New York, 1963.

Evans, Bertrand. *Shakespeare's Comedies*. New York, 1960.

Frye, Northrop. *Anatomy of Criticism: Four Essays*. Princeton, N. J., 1957.

Gohn, Ernest S. "Primitivistic Motifs in Sidney's *Arcadia*. PMASAL 45 (1960): 363-71.

Goldman, Marcus Seldon. *Sir Philip Sidney and the "Arcadia."* ISLL 17, nos. 1-2. Urbana, Ill., 1934.

Godshalk, Leigh, "Sidney's Revision of the *Arcadia*, Books III-V." *PQ* 43 (1964): 171-84.

Godshalk, William L. "Recent Studies in Sidney." *ELR* 2 (1972): 148-64.

Greenlaw, Edwin. "Sidney's *Arcadia* as an example of Elizabethan Allegory." *Kittredge Anniversary Papers*. Boston, 1913.

"The Captivity Episode in Sidney's 'Arcadia.' " The Manley Anniversary Studies. Chicago, 1923.

Greville, Fulke. The Life of the Renowned Sir Philip Sidney. Edited by Nowell Smith. Oxford, 1907.

Haller, William. "Hail Wedded Love." ELH 13 (1946): 79-97.

——— and Haller, Melleville. "The Puritan Art of Love." HLQ 5 (1942): 235-72.

Hamilton, A. C. "Recent Studies in the English Renaissance." SEL 9 (1969): 77.

——— "Sidney's Astrophel and Stella as a Sonnet Sequence." ELH 36 (1969): 59-87.

——— "Sidney's Arcadia as Prose Fiction: Its Relation to Its Sources." ELR 2 (1972): 29-60.

Heidegger, Martin. Sein und Zeit. Translated by John Macquarrie and Edward Robinson. New York, 1962.

Holland, Norman. The Dynamics of Literary Response. Oxford, 1968.

Isler, Alan D. "Heroic Poetry and Sidney's Two Arcadias." PMLA 83 1968): 368-79.

——— "Moral Philosophy and the Family in Sidney's Arcadia." HLQ 31 (1968): 359-71.

——— "Sidney, Shakespeare, and the 'Slain-Notslain.' " UTQ 37 (1967-68): 175-85.

Jones, Dorothy. "Sidney's Erotic Pen: An Interpretation of One of the Arcadia Poems." JEGP 73 (1974): 32-47.

Jusserand, J. J. The English Novel in the Time of Shakespeare. London, 1890; New York, 1966.

Kalstone, David. Sidney's Poetry: Contexts and Interpretations. Cambridge, Mass. 1965.

Kimbrough, Robert. Sir Philip Sidney. TEAS 114. New York, 1971.

Lanham, Richard A. The Old "Arcadia,," in Sidney's Arcadia. YSE 158. New Haven, Conn., 1965.

Lawry, Jon S. Sidney's Two Arcadias: Pattern and Proceeding. Ithaca, N. Y., 1972.

Levinson, Ronald. "The 'Godlesse Minde' in Sidney's Arcadia." MP 29 (1931): 21-26.

Lindenbaum, Peter. "Sidney's *Arcadia*: The Endings of the Three Versions." *HLQ* 34 (1971): 205-18.

Lindheim, Nancy Rothwax. "Sidney's *Arcadia*, Book II: Retrospective Narrative." *SP* 64 (1967): 159-86.

"Vision, Revision, and the 1593 Text of the *Arcadia*." *ELR* 2 (1972): 136-47.

Lovejoy, Arthur O., and Boas, George. *Primitivism and Related Ideas in Antiquity*. Baltimore, Md., 1935.

McKeithan, D. M. *"King Lear* and Sidney's *Arcadia." Texas Studies in English* 14 (1934): 45-49.

McNeir, Waldo F. "Trial by Combat in Elizabethan Literature." *NS* 15 (1966): 101-12.

McPherson, David C. "A Possible Origin for Mopsa in Sidney's *Arcadia."* *Renaissance Quarterly* 21 (1968): 420-28.

Marenco, Franco. *Arcadia Puritana: L'uso della tradizione nella prima "Arcadia" di Sir Philip Sidney*. Bari, 1968.

"Double Plot in Sidney's Old *Arcadia." MLR* 64 (1969): 248-63.

Meyerhoff, Hans. *Time in Literature*. Berkeley, Calif., 1955.

Myrick, Kenneth O. *Sir Philip Sidney as a Literary Craftsman*. Cambridge, Mass., 1939; Lincoln, Neb., 1965.

O'Connor, John J. *"Amadis de Gaule" and Its Influence on Elizabethan Literature*. New Brunswick, N. J., 1970.

Parker, Robert W. "Terentian Structure and Sidney's Original *Arcadia*." *ELR* 2 (1972): 61-78.

Patchell, Mary. *The Palmerin Romances in Elizabethan Prose Fiction*. New York, 1947.

Peele, George. *The Arraignment of Paris*. N.p., 1584.

Pellegrini, Angelo M. "Bruno, Sidney, and Spenser." *SP* 40 (1943): 128-44.

Pyle, Fitzroy. " 'Twelfth Night,' "King Lear' and 'Arcadia.' " *MLR* 43 (1948): 449-55.

Quinones, Ricardo J. *The Renaissance Discovery of Time*. Harvard Studies in Comparative Literature 31. Cambridge, Mass., 1972.

Rees, Joan. "Fulke Greville and the Revisions of *Arcadia*." *RES* 17 (1966): 54-57.

Ribner, Irving. "Machiavelli and Sidney: *The Arcadia of 1590.*" *SP* 47 (1950): 152-72.

———. "Sidney's *Arcadia* and the Structure of *King Lear.*" *Studia Neophilologica* 24 (1952): 63-68.

Rose, Mark. *Heroic Love: Studies in Sidney and Spenser.* Cambridge, Mass., 1968.

———. "Sidney's Womanish Man." *RES* 15 (1964): 353-63.

Rowe, Kenneth T. "The Countess of Pembroke's Editorship of the *Arcadia.*" *PMLA* 54 (1939): 122-38.

Rudenstein, Neil L. *Sidney's Poetic Development.* Cambridge, Mass., 1967.

Schleiner, Winfried. "Differences of Theme and Structure of the Erona Episode in the *Old* and *New Arcadia.*" *SP* 70 (1973): 377-91.

Shakespeare, William. *The Complete Works of Shakespeare.* Edited by Hardin Craig, Chicago, 1961.

Spenser, Edmund. *The Works: A Variorum Edition.* Edited by Edwin Greenlaw, *et al.* 9 vols. Baltimore, Md., 1932-1949.

Spingarn, J. E., ed. *Critical Essays of the Seventeenth Century.* Oxford, 1957; Bloomington, 1963.

Steadman, John M. " 'Meaning' and 'Name': Some Renaissance Interpretations of Urania." *NM* 64 (1963): 209-32.

Syford, Constance M. "The Direct Source of the Pamela-Cecropia Episode in the *Arcadia.*" *PMLA* 49 (1934): 472-89.

Thompson, Stith. *Motif-Index of Folk-Literature.* Rev. and enlarged ed. 6 vols. Bloomington, Ind., 1956.

Tillyard, E. M. W. *The English Epic and Its Background.* London, 1954; New York, 1966.

Toliver, Harold E. *Pastoral Forms and Attitudes.* Berkeley, Calif., 1971.

Townsend, Freda. "Sidney and Ariosto." *PMLA* 61 (1946): 97-108.

Turner, Myron. "The Disfigured Face of Nature: Image and Metaphor In the Revised *Arcadia.*" *ELR* 2 (1972): 116-35.

Walker, D. P. "Ways of Dealing with Atheists: A Background to Pamela's Refutation of Cecropia." *BHR* 17 (1955): 252-77.

Washington, Mary A. *Sir Philip Sidney: An Annotated Bibliography of Modern Criticism, 1941-1970.* Columbia, Mo., 1972.

Wild, John. *The Challenge of Existentialism.* Bloomington, Ind., 1955; 1966.

Wiles, A. G. D. "Parallel Analysis of the Two Versions of Sidney's *Arcadia.*" *SP* 39 (1942): 167-206.

Wolff, S. L. *The Greek Romances in Elizabethan Prose Fiction.* New York, 1912.

Woolf, Virginia. " 'The Countess of Pembroke's Arcadia.' " *The Second Common Reader.* New York, 1932; 1960.

Wright, Celeste Turner. "The Amazons in Elizabethan Literature." *SP* 37 (1940): 433-56.

Zandvoort, R. W. *Sidney's "Arcadia": A Comparison Between the Two Versions.* Amsterdam, 1929.

Index